Baseball

LIZABETH HARDMAN

LUCENT BOOKS
A part of Gale, Cengage Learning

Detroit • New York • San Francisco • New Haven, Conn • Waterville, Maine • London

LIBRARY OF CONGRESS CATALOGING-IN-PUBLICATION DATA

Hardman, Lizabeth.
  Baseball / by Lizabeth Hardman.
    p. cm. — (The science behind sports)
  Includes bibliographical references and index.
  ISBN 978-1-4205-0262-6 (hardcover)
1. Baseball—Juvenile literature. 2. Sports sciences—Juvenile literature. I. Title.
  GV867.5.H364 2010
  796.357—dc22

2010001601

Lucent Books
27500 Drake Rd
Farmington Hills MI 48331

ISBN-13: 978-1-4205-0262-6
ISBN-10: 1-4205-0262-X

Printed in the United States of America
2 3 4 5 6 7 14 13 12 11

Printed by Bang Printing, Brainerd, MN, 2nd Ptg., 05/2011

TABLE OF CONTENTS

On March 21, 1970, Slovenian ski jumper Vinko Bogataj took a terrible fall while competing at the Ski-flying World Championships in Oberstdorf, West Germany. Bogataj's pinwheeling crash was caught on tape by an ABC *Wide World of Sports* film crew and eventually became synonymous with "the agony of defeat" in competitive sporting. While many viewers were transfixed by the severity of Bogataj's accident, most were not aware of the biomechanical and environmental elements behind the skier's fall—heavy snow and wind conditions that made the ramp too fast and Bogataj's inability to maintain his center of gravity and slow himself down. Bogataj's accident illustrates that, no matter how mentally and physically prepared an athlete may be, scientific principles—such as momentum, gravity, friction, and aerodynamics—always have an impact on performance.

Lucent Book's Science Behind Sports series explores these and many more scientific principles behind some of the most popular team and individual sports, including baseball, hockey, gymnastics, wrestling, swimming, and skiing. Each volume in the series focuses on one sport or group of related sports. The volumes open with a brief look at the featured sport's origins, history and changes, then move on to cover the biomechanics and physiology of playing, related health and medical concerns, and the causes and treatment of sports-related injuries.

In addition to learning about the arc behind a curve ball, the impact of centripetal force on a figure skater, or how water buoyancy helps swimmers, Science Behind Sports readers will also learn how exercise, training, warming up, and diet and nutrition directly relate to peak performance and enjoyment of the sport. Volumes may also cover why certain sports are popular, how sports function in the business world, and which hot sporting issues—sports doping and cheating, for example—are in the news.

Basic physical science concepts, such as acceleration, kinetics, torque, and velocity, are explained in an engaging and accessible manner. The full-color text is augmented by fact boxes, sidebars, photos, and detailed diagrams, charts and graphs. In addition, a subject-specific glossary, bibliography and index provide further tools for researching the sports and concepts discussed throughout Science Behind Sports.

CHAPTER 1

America's Pastime—The Story of Baseball

Ask baseball fans why they love baseball, and they may have trouble putting it into words. Ernie Banks, Cubs legend and Hall of Famer, expresses it like this:

It's just life. When I think about baseball, it's just life. It's really the way life is. It requires a lot of mental capacity to be involved in it. It creates a lot of joy for people and memories for people who follow it. It's a family. You like it because it's a family. You started with it and know all these people—it's family, it's friends, it's fun, it's a beautiful game. All in all, baseball is amazing. I wish everybody could play it for at least two years. I wish everybody—men and women.[1]

One thing is certain—people who love baseball *really* love it, and they usually do for the rest of their lives. "The game gets inside you," says Eric Wedge, manager of the Cleveland Indians. "It becomes a part of who you are, and you don't know anything different. It's just something you feel passionate about. If you really feel that strong about something and you feel something that special, it's really hard to put it into words. For me, the love of the game is a given. It's been the one constant that I've known, for as far back as I can remember."[2]

Baseball and American Culture

Baseball has been an integral part of American culture since its beginnings in the early 1800s. Essayist Gerald Early says, "I think that there are only three things that America will be known for two thousand years from now when they study this civilization: the Constitution, jazz music, and baseball."[3] No fewer than forty movies have been made about baseball. Countless songs and poems have been written about baseball, including "Take Me Out to the Ballgame" and "Casey at the Bat."

Dozens of baseball expressions have become part of everyday American language. As Tristram Potter Coffin observed in *The Old Ball Game*, "The true test comes in the fact that old ladies who have never been to the ballpark, coquettes [young ladies] who don't know or care who's on first, men who think athletics begin and end with a pair of goal posts still know and use a great deal of baseball-derived terminology."[4] "Right off the bat," here are a few examples: If people do something wrong, they have "dropped the ball," but if they do something right, they are "still in the game," and, if they do it right every time, they are "batting a thousand." At work, people try to be "team players," but if they are a little strange, they are "out in left field." Most people have "gone to bat in a pinch" for friends who have "two strikes against them." If people are waiting their turn at something, they are "on deck." If they are estimating something, they might give a "ballpark figure." And when making important plans, people always try to "cover all the bases."

As adults, many people feel as if they relive their childhood by going to a ball game and possibly passing on their love of the game to their own children. Baseball can help people relive a time when life was simpler. It can be a source of comfort and security for many people. Perhaps no other time in American history has baseball provided as much a source of consolation and strength as in the days after September 11, 2001. Only seven weeks after the terrorist attacks on New York City, the

A giant American flag is displayed right before Game One of the 2001 World Series played soon after the 9-11 terrorists attacks. The game of baseball helped the nation to heal after such a tragic event in the country's history.

World Series took place there between the New York Mets and the Arizona Diamondbacks. For many Americans, the World Series being played in New York by a team from New York was a perfect and fitting demonstration of the strength of the people of the United States and their determination to carry on with their way of life, even in the face of profound tragedy, and it provided a much-needed boost in morale for the beleaguered citizens of New York.

The Beginnings of Baseball

Baseball may be called America's national pastime, but its beginnings lie elsewhere in the world. Games similar to baseball have been played in many countries over the centuries. A Romanian game of "oina" is similar to baseball in that a ball is thrown to a batter who tries to hit it as far as possible and then runs back and forth between bases before the ball is brought back from the field. "Lapta" is a Russian ball-and-bat game that has been played since at least the fourteenth century. Germany has a game called "schlagball" (shock ball), in which a bowler (the pitcher) tosses a ball to a striker (the batter), who hits it with a club and then tries to run around the bases before a fielder can hit the striker with the ball. The game that Americans call baseball, however, evolved mostly from early folk games played in England.

English Folk Games

The first known mention of baseball in print appears in a book called *A Little Pretty Pocket-Book*, published in England in 1744. The book contains a short poem called "Base-Ball," accompanied by a picture of people playing a game of stoolball, a fourteenth-century English folk game. In stoolball a batter stood in front of a target, often a tree stump or a stool turned upside down. The pitcher threw the ball at the target, and the batter tried to defend the target by hitting the ball away with either a bat or a bare hand. If the ball hit the stool, the batter was out. In some versions, no running was involved. In others the batter might run between two stools or around several stools.

Cricket is a very old game, still popular in England, and also believed to have contributed to the development of baseball. In cricket two runners stand at either end of a 58-foot- (17.68m-) long rectangle called the "pitch." Each runner stands next to a wicket—three poles stuck close together in the ground, topped by two wooden pieces called "bails." The wicket serves as a target, as in stoolball. One runner is the striker, or batsman. A bowler, or pitcher, throws the ball as hard as possible toward the striker. When the striker hits the ball, both runners run to the other end of the pitch, which scores a run. Meanwhile, the fielders try to catch the ball and throw it in to break the wicket before the runner can get back to it.

Rounders is another English game that is related to baseball, except that the pitcher and the batter are on the same team, runners run clockwise, the batter is out whether the ball is caught on the fly or on a bounce, and runners are out if the fielder hits them with the ball. In the early 1800s, Americans played a version

BATTER'S BOX

Over 100

Number of slang words for "hit," such as "blooper," "Texas Leaguer," "bleeder," "nibbler," "scratch," "seeing eye," and "squib."

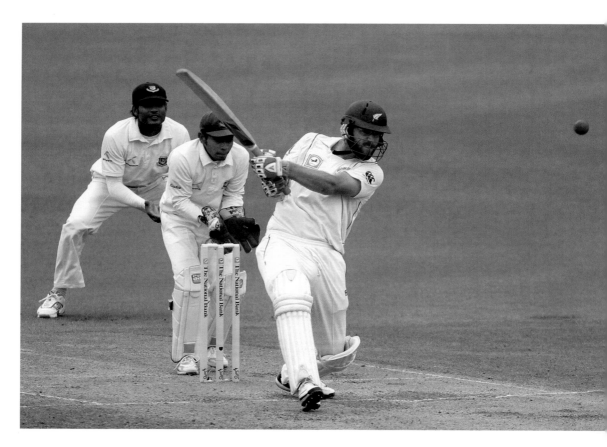

of rounders that they called "town ball." In both games, as in baseball, three strikes and the batter is out.

Baseball Gets Its Own Rules

Although baseball seems to be related to both cricket and rounders, the actual origins of the American game are not clear. Some baseball historians believe that baseball and town ball evolved separately from one another. Others believe that baseball had nothing to do with either cricket or rounders, and that it is a purely American invention. One fact is certain: the first official rules for baseball were written in 1845 for a New York City baseball club called the Knickerbockers. They were called the "Knickerbocker Rules."

The man who wrote the Knickerbocker rules was a New Yorker named Alexander J. Cartwright. Many people consider him the "Father of Baseball." In the late 1840s Cartwright became caught up in the California Gold Rush. As he traveled West, he introduced his version of the game to many of the cities through which he passed. In 1953 Congress officially declared him to be the true inventor of modern baseball, and he is in the Baseball Hall of Fame in Cooperstown, New York.

Baseball Becomes Professional

In 1846 the first organized game between two baseball clubs took place in Hoboken, New Jersey, between the Knickerbockers and the New York Nine. In 1857 the National Association of Base Ball Players (NABBP) was formed as the first organization to govern the rules of baseball. Sixteen ball clubs met and rewrote the Knickerbocker Rules. By 1865 more than one hundred clubs belonged to the NABBP, and more than four hundred had joined by 1867.

Baseball was beginning to catch on with the public, and clubs began to build their own parks, charge admission to the games, and pay their players. In 1869 the Cincinnati Red Stockings became the first fully professional baseball team, followed by the Boston Red Stockings in 1871. In 1870 conflicts between professional and amateur ball clubs resulted in the formation of the National Association of Professional Base Ball Players (NAPBBP). The NAPBBP lasted until 1875, when the National League of Professional Base Ball Clubs was formed. The National League included only teams from larger cities who were more competitive and financially strong. It imposed rules that prevented players from going to other teams for more pay and required teams to play all scheduled games, even if they were out of the running for the league championship. About this time both organizations agreed (unofficially) to exclude black players from professional baseball. Several black players already on teams were dropped from the rosters.

Smaller regional baseball associations existing at the time formed the roots of today's minor league system. In 1900 one of these minor leagues, the

BATTER'S BOX

10 years old

The age of Catcher Edith "The Kid" Houghton when she joined the Philadelphia Bobbies in 1922.

MAJOR LEAGUE BASEBALL TODAY

Today, Major League Baseball consists of two leagues each broken into three divisions – east, central, and west. The American League contains fourteen teams; the National League has sixteen teams.

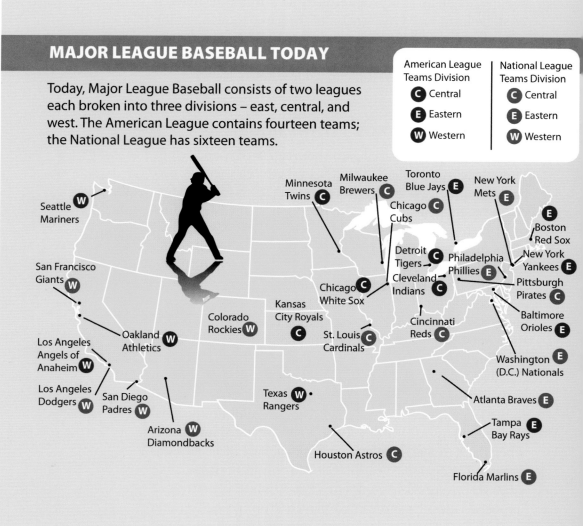

American League Teams Division
- **C** Central
- **E** Eastern
- **W** Western

National League Teams Division
- **C** Central
- **E** Eastern
- **W** Western

Seattle Mariners **W**

Minnesota Twins **C**

Milwaukee Brewers **C**

Toronto Blue Jays **E**

New York Mets **E**

Chicago Cubs **C**

E Boston Red Sox

San Francisco Giants **W**

Detroit Tigers **C**

Philadelphia Phillies **E**

New York Yankees **E**

Cleveland Indians **C**

Pittsburgh Pirates **C**

Chicago White Sox **C**

Kansas City Royals **C**

Baltimore Orioles **E**

Colorado Rockies **W**

St. Louis Cardinals **C**

Cincinnati Reds **C**

Los Angeles Angels of Anaheim **W**

Oakland Athletics **W**

Washington (D.C.) Nationals **E**

Los Angeles Dodgers **W**

San Diego Padres **W**

Texas Rangers **W**

Atlanta Braves **E**

Arizona Diamondbacks **W**

Tampa Bay Rays **E**

Houston Astros **C**

Florida Marlins **E**

Western League, decided to challenge the National League's dominance and became the American League. They competed with the National League by attracting players away with better contracts. The rest of the small league teams banded together and earned income by selling players to the two major leagues. Eventually, most minor league teams became associated with a major league team. Today, the minor leagues provide a place for younger players to earn a living while improving their skills, with the hope of eventually moving up to a major league team.

The "Black Sox" Scandal

Chicago White Sox owner Charles Comiskey was one of the most despised owners in baseball. In 1919 the Sox were the best team in baseball, but they were also the lowest paid. Comiskey frequently made promises he never intended to keep. After promising pitcher Eddie Cicotte a $10,000 bonus if he won thirty games, Comiskey benched him after he won his twenty-ninth. He tried to make the players pay for laundering their uniforms, and, when they refused, he had the uniforms laundered and then fined the players.

These and other behaviors created resentment among the players, so several of them decided to "fix" (lose on purpose) the World Series that year. The players deliberately made mistakes so that the White Sox would lose, and professional gamblers would make money by betting on the other team, the Cincinnati Reds. Since the Sox were heavily favored to win, betting against them would earn the gamblers a lot of money. The gamblers agreed to pay $100,000 to the players who participated in the fix.

The Reds won the World Series, but the unusually bad play by the White Sox did not go unnoticed. Rumors flew that the series had been fixed. In 1920 a grand jury was convened to investigate, but, after important evidence went missing, the players were found not guilty of fixing the games. However, because the reputation of baseball had been ruined, Federal Judge Kenesaw Mountain Landis, the first commissioner of baseball, banned eight White Sox players, including Shoeless Joe Jackson, from ever playing baseball again. A few of them tried to clear their names, but none of the eight were ever reinstated in major league baseball. The last of them died in 1975.

York Times.

WEDNESDAY, SEPTEMBER 29, 1920   TWO CENTS

EIGHT WHITE SOX PLAYERS ARE INDICTED ON CHARGE OF FIXING 1919 WORLD SERIES; CICOTTE GOT $10,000 AND JACKSON $5,000

Yankee Owners Give Praise to Comiskey And Offer Him Use of Their Whole Team

COMISKEY SUSPENDS THEM

Promises to Run Them Out of Baseball if

A front page headline from the New York Times *describing the "Black Sox" scandal in which players for the Chicago White Sox intentionally lost the 1919 World Series.*

Baseball in the Twentieth Century

The first twenty years of the twentieth century are commonly known as the "dead ball era" in baseball. Games were low scoring, and strategies focused on singles, bunts, stealing bases, and other "small ball" methods. Despite power hitters such as Honus Wagner and Ty Cobb, home runs were rare, and pitchers dominated the game. One reason for this is that, at that time, baseballs were expensive, so one ball might be used the entire game. By the end it could be covered with mud, grass, and other substances such as spit and tobacco juice. Balls in this condition were hard to see, and, thus, hard to hit out of the park. The dead ball era ended in 1920, because of one rule change and one player.

In 1920 Cleveland Indian Ray Chapman was hit in the head by a pitch and died the next day. Because of this, major league baseball instituted the rule that umpires must remove a ball from a game if it becomes dirty and hard to see, if the pitcher applies any substance to it, such as spit, that causes an "unnatural flight" through the air, or if it becomes scuffed or damaged. With the ball easier to see and with pitchers forbidden to alter the natural flight of the ball, batters hit more home runs.

At about the same time, Red Sox pitcher George Herman "Babe" Ruth was switched to the outfield so that he could bring his considerable hitting talent to the game every day instead of only every four days, as pitchers do not play every day. In his last season with the Red Sox, he hit twenty-nine home runs. The next year, as a Yankee, he hit fifty-four, and in 1921 he hit fifty-nine. In 1927 he hit sixty home runs, a record that lasted until 1961. The dead ball era was over.

Fans loved the "long ball." Clubs modified their parks to make home runs easier. Every team made sure to sign their own "slugger." Hitting, rather than pitching, came to dominate the game, and power hitters such as Babe Ruth, Rogers Hornsby, Lou Gehrig, Jimmie Foxx, and Hack Wilson became America's heroes. Baseball came to the radio waves in 1921, allowing those who could not get to a game to catch baseball fever. Attendance at games rose steadily until the Great Depression hit in 1929. Then came World War II, and many players went to war. Baseball continued, however, with players such as Ted Williams, Joe DiMaggio, and Stan Musial making headlines. Right after the war, baseball experienced another milestone when the color barrier was finally broken.

The Negro Leagues

By the late 1800s, in response to being excluded from major league baseball, African Americans had formed their own professional teams. The first black professional baseball team, the Babylon Black Panthers, was formed in 1885. White businessman Walter Cook sponsored them and, because the country of Cuba was on good terms with the United States at the time, he renamed the team the Cuban Giants, hoping to attract more white spectators.

In 1917 the United States entered World War I. The need for workers in the defense industry attracted a great number of African American southerners to the northern states. With a larger fan base, the push was on to start a new Negro baseball league. In 1920 the Negro National League was formed with eight teams. The first league game was played on May 2, 1920. Other Negro leagues formed as well, but largely due to the Great Depression, almost all of them had folded by the early 1930s.

In 1933 a known gangster named Gus Greenlee decided to start a new seven-team league. He already owned a team that included two of the most famous black players, Satchel Paige and Josh Gibson.

The Kansas City Monarchs, one of the Negro League teams, pose for a team photo before a game in Denver, Colorado, in 1934.

He gave his league the earlier name, the Negro National League. In 1937 the Negro American League joined Greenlee's league. In 1942 they held the Negro League World Series.

After the major leagues became integrated in 1947, interest in the Negro leagues faded. Promising young black players signed with major league teams, and players who already had contracts with Negro league teams abandoned them for the majors. The Negro National League folded in 1948, followed by the Negro American League in 1958.

Breaking the Color Barrier

As baseball was developing into a professional sport, America was still very much a racially segregated country. After 1888 African Americans were not accepted into either the major or minor leagues. In 1920 the Negro

National League (NNL) was founded so that African Americans could play professional baseball. The Negro American League (NAL) followed in 1937. After World War II, the Commissioner of Major League Baseball, Happy Chandler, felt that it was wrong to exclude blacks from major league baseball when they had fought for their country along with white soldiers. Branch Rickey, then the general manager of the Brooklyn Dodgers, sent scouts all over the country to find a black player who would be mentally and emotionally strong enough to break the color barrier. They found one in the NNL team the Kansas City Monarchs—a shortstop named Jackie Robinson.

Women Step Up to the Plate

By 1942 World War II had taken so many young men that many minor league teams were forced to disband. Ballpark owners feared that their parks would have to close, so a substitute had to be found. In 1943 Chicago Cubs owner Philip K. Wrigley founded the All-American Girls Softball League. Hundreds of women showed up to try out for the new teams. Sixty young women, some as young as fifteen, were chosen as the first female professional baseball players.

Four teams started spring training that year, and league play began in May. The women's game was a blend of softball and baseball. Their uniforms included a flared skirt, satin shorts, knee-high socks, and a ball cap. They played 108 games, followed by a championship series. The first season was considered a success, with more than 176,000 fans attending the games. The next

season, two more teams were added, and by the end of the 1945 season, attendance had risen to more than 450,000. Women's baseball continued to flourish even after the war ended, with more than 900,000 fans attending in 1948.

The women's game went through several changes until, by the 1950s, the word "Softball" in the league's name had been changed to "Baseball," and the game was now essentially the same as the men's. It became difficult to find women talented enough to play the more rigorous and demanding game. Also in the 1950s, other forms of entertainment, along with the arrival of televised men's games, led to a decline in interest in women's baseball. In 1952 Commissioner of Major League Baseball Ford Frick banned the signing of women to professional baseball contracts. The women's league ended in 1954.

Rickey gave Robinson a "test," in which he yelled at Robinson and hurled racial slurs at him to see if he could tolerate what black players would hear during games. Robinson passed the test and was offered a contract to play with the Dodgers. In April 1947 Robinson made his debut in major league baseball. He was named Rookie of the Year and became the first black player inducted into the Baseball Hall of Fame.

From National Pastime to World Pastime

Since the 1980s baseball's popularity has extended beyond the borders of the United States and has spread around the world. Two Canadian cities—Toronto and Montreal—formed major league teams, and every American team has players from countries such as the Dominican Republic, Japan, Cuba, Australia, Colombia, Holland, South Korea, Taiwan, and Venezuela. One reason for this is that major league baseball has become an extremely high-paying profession, which makes it a very attractive career option for talented young men. Also, the expansion process means that more teams have been added to the major leagues, all of which need full rosters. Finding quality players, especially pitchers, is more difficult if recruitment is limited to only North and South America.

Not only are foreign players coming to America to play, baseball itself has gone overseas. The first baseball games played outside the United States were played in England 1874, and an 1888 tour took baseball to countries in Africa, in Europe, and around the Pacific. Today, baseball organizations exist in countries as diverse as Japan, Ireland, Belgium, Sweden, Italy, Finland, Croatia, and many others. Baseball became an official Olympic Sport in 1992, and in 2006 major league baseball established the World Baseball Classic, a highly publicized international baseball tournament.

BATTER'S BOX
Speaking Japanese
In Japan, "baseball" is "besuboru," and "three strikes" is "suree suturaikku."

Japanese baseball fans show their team spirit after a game between Japan and the United States during the 2009 World Baseball Classic in Los Angeles, California. The World Baseball Classic is a highly publicized international tournament.

Not As Simple As It Looks

Since its beginnings, baseball has evolved from a simple bat-and-ball game into a complicated, intricate game. Most baseball fans will say that it is well worth the effort of learning about it. As Joe Kweskin, a Chicago White Sox fan, says:

It's unique unto itself. Football, basketball and hockey are variations of the same concept—back and forth ... to score a goal. Baseball, however, is mapped out on the field unlike any other sport. A running back ... can run 100 yards, tops; a base runner legging out an inside-the-park homer runs 20 yards farther. Baseball is the most democratic of sports—any size can play, and because the ball is not controlled by the offense but rather the defense, every player at any given time is involved in a play. Along with the ... premise that hitting a pitched baseball is the single most difficult thing to do in sports, so might be fielding a 175-mph line drive or grounder down the line. I love baseball because it is the greatest game ever invented.[5]

Maybe that's why, whenever baseball fans hear the "Star-Spangled Banner," they can hardly resist the urge to follow it with a shout of "Play ball!"

CHAPTER 2

Power Hitters and Cannon Arms— Training and Conditioning

Baseball players, like high-level athletes of any sport, go through extensive physical training and conditioning programs that are specifically designed to develop skills needed for baseball. Training and conditioning for baseball focuses on developing strength, power, speed, quickness, agility, and flexibility. Proper nutrition is also very important in athletic conditioning.

Strength Training for Baseball

Before the 1980s strength training was not an important part of conditioning for a baseball player. People viewed baseball as a game of skill and finesse rather than strength, and most managers and coaches saw strength training as something for body builders, not baseball players. They feared that weight lifting and building large muscles would cause players to become "muscle-bound" and interfere with quickness and proper technique. Today, strength training is recognized as necessary for developing superior speed, endurance, and power. Tony Burtt, of Cutting Edge Training for Athletes, says, "A baseball training program should incorporate a strength training component. Strength is crucial for baseball success."[6] It is not so much about body building, in which the main goal is to build the muscles as large as possible. Big muscles are not necessarily stronger muscles, and in baseball, muscle strength is more important than muscle size.

How Muscles Work

The human body is composed of three different types of muscles. Cardiac muscle is the muscle of the heart. Smooth muscle makes up the walls of the body's hollow organs, such as the stomach, bladder, and intestines. The skeletal muscle is involved in strength training.

Skeletal muscles are attached to the bones by tough, whitish bands called tendons. Contraction, or shortening, of skeletal muscle is what makes movement possible. A good example of this is the muscles of the upper arm—the biceps on the front and the triceps on the back—which allow a person to bend and straighten the elbow. When a person wants to bend at the elbow, the brain sends a message to the biceps, which contracts and pulls on the tendon to pull the forearm up at the elbow. When the person wants to straighten that arm, the brain sends a message to the triceps on the back of the upper arm. When the triceps contracts, it pulls the forearm down and the arm straightens. Every such movement of the body depends on the contraction of a muscle.

Skeletal muscles are complex structures. A skeletal muscle, such as the biceps, is made up of thousands of long muscle cells, or fibers, which run the length of the muscle. Groups of muscle fibers work together with a motor neuron, a nerve that makes the group of fibers contract during movement. The group of fibers along with its motor neuron is called a "motor unit."

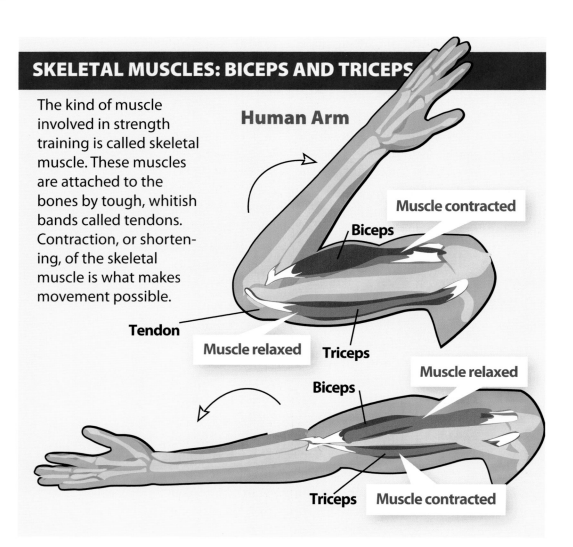

SKELETAL MUSCLES: BICEPS AND TRICEPS

The kind of muscle involved in strength training is called skeletal muscle. These muscles are attached to the bones by tough, whitish bands called tendons. Contraction, or shortening, of the skeletal muscle is what makes movement possible.

Human Arm

Muscle contracted

Biceps

Tendon

Muscle relaxed

Triceps

Muscle relaxed

Biceps

Triceps

Muscle contracted

There are two basic types of muscle fibers. Slow-twitch (ST) fibers contract slowly and do not grow as big, but they do not tire quickly. They are used for movements that require less power and more endurance. Fast twitch (FT) fibers contract faster and can grow larger, but also tire sooner. Athletes whose muscles contain more fast-twitch fibers excel at sports in which shorter bursts of energy are needed. "There is great variability in the percentage of fiber types among athletes," says exercise physiologist Jason Karp. "For example, it is well-known that endurance athletes have a greater proportion of slow-twitch fibers, while sprinters and jumpers have more fast-twitch fibers."[7] Baseball players need to produce energy in shorter, stronger bursts, so the successful ones tend to have more fast-twitch fibers in their muscles.

Power Training

In the same way that athletes can be quite muscular but lack the corresponding amount of strength, they can also be strong but lack power. Power is closely related to strength, but power also includes speed of movement. Power means that an athlete can use the maximum amount of strength in the shortest possible period of time. Baseball players must be able to generate explosive power for skills such as hitting the ball hard, pitching a good fastball, and getting from one base to the next as swiftly as possible. The concept of power can be expressed in a formula called the "Force-Velocity Relationship":

$$\text{Power} = \text{Force} \times \frac{\text{Distance}}{\text{Time}}$$

In this equation, "force" is how much strength is applied to move the weight. "Distance" is how far the athlete must move the weight, whether it be a full swing of the bat or the distance between two bases. "Time" is the length of time it takes to move the weight through the distance. Strength training increases the "force" component of the formula. Power training aims to decrease the time part of the formula, so that the athlete can apply strength through the full distance of the movement in the shortest possible time.

To develop explosive power, an athlete's first goal must be to achieve maximum strength for each muscle group being trained. A commonly used statistic is the athlete's 1RM, which stands for "one rep maximum." The 1RM is the most weight a muscle can move in one repetition. Once the athlete has determined the 1RM for a muscle, training focuses on the time part of the Force-Velocity Relationship. Research has shown that moving weight loads that are about 75 to 85 percent of the 1RM is the best way to shorten

BATTER'S BOX
Water
About 75 percent of skeletal muscle and about 80 percent of the human brain is comprised of this substance.

How Muscles Get Stronger

When people lift weights, they place stress on the muscle fibers to move the weight. The stress of moving heavy weights causes microscopic damage to the muscle fibers. Several things happen in response to the damage. First, other cells that are part of the immune system release chemicals called "cytokines," which cause inflammation and muscle soreness. Second, the body sends increased amounts of fluid and blood to the muscle to help it heal. The damaged fibers also help themselves heal by releasing chemicals that stimulate cell growth. Then, if the athlete allows some time for the muscle to rest, the fibers will become larger and split into new fibers, adding size and strength to the muscle. Allowing the muscle to rest until the soreness is gone is important because without it, the fibers can be torn, the muscle can become weak, and the athlete can become injured.

A muscle also gets larger by recruiting, or activating, new motor units in

It is important to let muscles rest after lifting weights. This allows damaged fibers to heal and to become larger by splitting into new fibers.

response to the increased demands of prolonged, intense exercise. During exercise, smaller slow-twitch motor units are recruited first, followed by the larger fast-twitch motor units. The more intense the workout, the more large fast-twitch motor units are recruited. Over time, the muscle gets larger as more large motor units are recruited.

the time part of the equation and increase power. For example, a person who can do one squat with 200 pounds (90.72kg) of weight might train for power by doing three to five squats with 150 to 170 pounds (68.04 to 77.11kg). Moving weights heavier than 85 percent of the 1RM may build strength, but will not develop power as effectively because it limits the athlete's ability to move the weight quickly.

Ballistics and Plyometrics

One training method designed for developing power is ballistics. Ballistics works by forcing an athlete's muscles to recruit more fast-twitch muscle fibers. In ballistics, high amounts of force are applied to low amounts of resistance, or weight, so that the movement is rapid. Unlike traditional weight lifting, in which a majority of the movement is involved with slowing and stopping the movement of the weight, ballistics allows the athlete to move the resistance quickly throughout the entire range of the movement so as not to expend energy to slow and stop the movement. An example of a ballistic exercise is throwing a weighted ball called a medicine ball. The athlete must apply great force to throw the ball but does not expend any energy to stop the movement because the ball leaves his hands at the end of the movement. This increases power in throwing.

Another training method for power is plyometrics. Plyometrics has its beginnings in the training programs of Eastern European athletes in the 1970s. Donald A. Chu, author of *Jumping into Plyometrics*, explains, "As the Eastern bloc countries [countries formerly part of the Soviet Union, such as Romania, Poland, East Germany, and Czechoslovakia] began to produce superior athletes in such sports as track and field, gymnastics, and weightlifting, the mystique of their success began to center on their training methods. Plyometrics rapidly became known to coaches and athletes as exercises or drills aimed at linking strength with speed of movement to produce power."[8]

Plyometrics is similar to ballistics except that in plyometrics, the muscle is put into a lengthening pre-stretch, or eccentric action, before being put into a contracting, or concentric action, as force is applied to the resistance. A muscle that is lengthened just before contracting will contract more forcefully and more quickly, like a spring or a rubber band that is stretched out before being allowed to snap back to its original position.

Plyometric exercises have three phases. Together, the three phases comprise the stretch-shortening cycle. The first phase is the eccentric action. In this phase, energy is

BATTER'S BOX

106

The number of bones, out of 206 in the human body, which are located in the hands and feet.

created and stored in the muscle. Second is the period of time between the eccentric action and the beginning of the contraction. The shorter this time is, the more forceful the contraction will be. The third phase is the actual contraction of the muscle. An example of a plyometric exercise is the squat jump. A person can jump much higher and with more force by crouching into a squat (eccentric action) immediately before jumping upward (concentric action). Power is developed in the legs by doing repetitive squat jumps, especially if the second phase—the time between squat and jump—is very brief.

Developing Speed, Quickness, and Agility

Strength and power both contribute to developing another skill set necessary in baseball—speed and quickness. The goals of speed training are to maximize velocity (how fast the athlete can cover a particular distance), maintain that velocity as the muscles fatigue later in the game, and increase acceleration (how quickly an athlete reaches his maximum speed).

Quickness is related to speed, but is not the same thing. Quickness refers to how quickly athletes can react to situations and move appropriately, how rapidly they can stop after accelerating, and how well they can suddenly change direction and maintain balance. Training for speed and quickness is critical in baseball for skills such as running the bases, fielding a sharply hit grounder, and getting into position to catch a fly ball.

The running that a baseball player does is mostly done in short sprints, rather than over long distances. Training for speed and quickness therefore focuses on developing quick starts, rapid acceleration, and quick stops. Long periods of slow jogging do little to develop speed and quickness, but sprint training helps an athlete shorten his reaction time, reach his top speed quickly, and stop on a dime. Running sprints on uphill and downhill slopes increases strength and power in the legs. Short, fast sprints between two cones or bases develop the ability to stop and change direction quickly.

Science Changes Baseball—The Steroid Era

Beginning in the 1980s, training and conditioning for baseball changed dramatically. Weight training, strict conditioning, and more emphasis on diet resulted in baseball players who were bigger, stronger, and faster than ever before. As superior athletic performance began to translate into multimillion-dollar contracts, players looked for ways to gain a competitive edge and make themselves more valuable. Some players, including some in college and even high school, resorted to taking anabolic steroids, performance-enhancing drugs that increased their body size and strength very rapidly, as well as decreased the time needed to recover from injury.

Anabolic steroids are synthetic, or man-made, forms of the male hormone testosterone. They have been used in medicine since the 1930s to treat abnormal growth as well as illnesses that cause muscle wasting, such as cancer and AIDS. When combined with weight training and proper diet, they can increase muscle mass and strength. With long-term use, however, they can cause abnormally aggressive behavior ("roid rage") and serious health problems such as high blood pressure, liver damage, and heart disease.

BALCO Labs, the company that in 2002 produced undetectable steroids thought to be used by many professional athletes, including professional baseball players.

Steroids were banned from use in baseball in 1991, but the ban went largely unheeded and unenforced. In 2002 it was discovered that a company called BALCO had been manufacturing steroids in forms that were undetectable by traditional drug tests. In 2006 Congress began an investigation into the illegal use of steroids by professional baseball players. Its final report named eighty-nine players suspected to have used steroids or other illegal performance-enhancing drugs. In response major league baseball instituted tougher measures to prevent illegal drug use by professional baseball players.

Agility is closely related to and necessary for speed and quickness. Agility is the athlete's ability to move his body, especially his arms, legs, and back, quickly in any direction without injuring the tissues involved in those movements.

Agility allows an infielder to dive for a ground ball, get quickly to his feet, and fire the ball to first base, or for a first baseman to scoop a bad throw out of the dirt and still keep one foot on the bag. "When it comes to baseball, speed and agility are important on both sides of the field," says trainer and coach Charles Slavik. "Speed is important in the field where hit balls must be defended. On offense, speed puts pressure on the other team and distracts the pitcher and catcher; this helps the hitter get better pitches to hit. The development of speed and agility is as vital as the development of batting power and throwing arm stability."[9]

Flexibility

Flexibility measures how far an athlete can move a joint without pain—his range of motion (ROM). Flexibility is important because muscles, tendons, and ligaments (tissues that hold the bones together inside the joint) that are too tight restrict joint movement and decrease speed and agility. A lack of flexibility also increases the risk of injuries, especially in male athletes.

Several factors influence flexibility. The particular structure of each joint determines how far and in what directions it can move. For example, a hinge joint such as a finger or knee can only move up or down, and once it is straight, it cannot move any farther without injury. The wrist can move up and down, side to side, or around in circles. The ball and socket joint of the shoulder has the most movement options of all the joints. Older people tend to be less flexible than younger people, and men tend to be less flexible than women. Very large muscles can inhibit flexibility because their size interferes with the joint's ability to move through its full ROM. Internal environment of the body affects ROM. For example, muscles and joints are less flexible when a person first gets out of bed in the morning, or when body temperature is low. Previous injuries can also limit flexibility because injured tissues become scarred and thickened, or fibrosed, as they heal. Fibrosed tissues cannot stretch as well as normal, uninjured tissues.

Stretching

Training for agility and flexibility includes stretching exercises that allow the muscles and joints to move through their maximum ROM without damage. Stretching is an important part of the warm-up for any exercise program because it helps prevent injury during the exercise.

Professional baseball player Edgar Renteria performs some walking lunges before a 2009 game in Philadelphia. Walking lunges is just one example of dynamic stretching.

Several different stretching exercises, each with its own purpose in agility and flexibility training, can be used. Static stretching involves slow, constant stretching of a muscle to its maximum stretch and then holding it there for twenty to thirty seconds. Static stretching can be active, in which the person provides the force to hold the stretch, or passive, in which a partner or machine provides the force to stretch the muscle. Over time, static stretching increases range of motion of the joints and improves speed and jumping ability.

Many coaches believe that static stretching should only be done as a cool-down after exercise is completed rather than as part of the pre-exercise warm-up. They prefer dynamic stretching for the warm-up. Dynamic stretching elongates the muscles using constant movement rather than holding the muscles still. Examples of dynamic stretches are arm circles, walking lunges, and leg swings. Dynamic stretching is also helpful for preventing muscle tightness after exercise.

Ballistic stretching is similar to dynamic stretching except that ballistic stretching adds a series of bounces to the end of the stretch to increase the range of the stretch. An example is a toe touch with a series of short bounces at the end. Ballistic stretching does help to increase range of motion, but it must be done in a carefully controlled fashion, otherwise there is a risk of sudden overstretching and potential injury to the muscle.

Nutrition and Training

None of the training methods already discussed can be effective without proper nutrition. All of the skills needed to play baseball depend on providing enough of the right fuel for the body so that the athlete maintains strength, stamina, and mental alertness throughout the game. Nutrients important for baseball players include carbohydrates, proteins, and plenty of fluids, especially water.

Carbohydrate is the fuel that the body uses to generate energy for everyday bodily functions, such as breathing and digestion, and for fueling the muscles during exercise. Baseball players need a fairly high intake of carbohydrate, about

50 to 60 percent of their diet, to maintain their stamina, especially during training periods.

The two main kinds of carbohydrate are simple and complex. Simple carbohydrate is quickly digested and is found in foods that have high amounts of sugars, such as candy and other sweets, many fruits, milk, and white bread. The energy it provides tends to be short lasting. Complex carbohydrate takes longer to digest. It is found in foods such as whole grain breads, cereals, pasta, and vegetables. Complex carbohydrate is considered to be better for a training diet because it is found in foods that have more valuable nutrients and because the energy it provides is more long lasting than that provided by simple carbohydrate.

The second major nutrient important for training is protein. Scientists estimated that more than 50 percent of human body weight is protein. Proteins are everywhere in the body—in muscle, bone, brain cells, blood, and many

Whether a professional player or little leaguer, all baseball players should keep hydrated during a game to avoid serious health problems, such as heat stroke.

other body tissues. Lean protein such as that found in poultry, fish, eggs, cottage cheese, and lean red meats provides the nutrients necessary for muscles to repair themselves after intense exercise. When protein is digested, it is broken down into smaller "building blocks" called "amino acids." The amino acids are then built back into protein and used to build and repair damaged tissues and reinforce muscle fibers, a process called "muscle-protein synthesis." Adequate protein intake, combined with proper exercise and rest, helps muscles reach and maintain their healthiest condition.

A third component to proper nutritional conditioning is adequate intake of fluids during exercise periods. The body needs fluids, especially water, to carry out all its functions and to maintain normal body temperature. Baseball is an outdoor sport, played in spring and summer, when temperatures are often high, so the body can lose a significant amount of water, especially from sweating. Sweating also causes the loss of electrolytes, essential chemicals that keep the body's systems functioning, especially the nerves, heart, and muscles. They make sweat taste a little salty. The loss of even small amounts of water and electrolytes can affect athletes' stamina and ability to maintain focus and concentration. Serious health problems, such as heat stroke, can result from inadequate replacement of lost fluids. Athletes must drink plenty of fluids, such as sports drinks, that replace water, carbohydrates, and electrolytes.

CHAPTER 3

Tommy John Elbow—Baseball Injuries

Training and conditioning go a long way toward preventing injuries associated with playing baseball. Still, baseball players can and do get injured, and a severe injury can end a player's career. Baseball, because of the way it is played, lends itself to certain injuries that are more common in baseball than in other sports. Prompt, effective treatment of injuries when they happen is the best way to get the player back out on the field. Baseball injuries, like injuries in most other sports, can be classified as either overuse injuries, also called cumulative injuries, or acute traumatic injuries.

Overuse Injuries

Overuse injuries, as the name implies, are injuries that happen because of repetitive use of a body part over a long period of time without allowing sufficient time for the body part to heal between episodes of stress. Muscles, ligaments, and tendons can adapt to long-term stress, but if stresses are placed on the tissues too frequently, damage happens faster than rebuilding, so the tissues cannot heal, and they become stiffened with scar tissue and become less flexible.

Overuse injuries can happen for many reasons. They may occur at the beginning of a new workout program, and if the athlete is over anxious and does too much too soon. They may happen to an athlete who believes that if a little is good, more is better, and does not allow adequate healing time between workouts. They can happen if an injured athlete tries to resume playing before an injury has fully healed. Overuse injuries can result from poor form, improperly fitted shoes, or inappropriate equipment during workouts or games. Even experienced athletes who have been playing their sports for a long time can get an overuse injury if they increase their training suddenly for some reason. Doing only one kind of exercise over and over again can also lead to an overuse injury.

Diagnosis of an overuse injury can often be made simply by listening to the athlete's description of his symptoms and activity schedule. Symptoms of an overuse injury usually begin with minor pain and stiffness that may interfere with use of the part. Numbness, tingling, or swelling can also occur if nerves or blood vessels are involved. In some cases, X-rays or other tests may be needed, especially if surgery is being considered as a treatment.

Without adequate treatment, overuse injuries get worse, become more painful, and can prevent the athlete from using the affected part. If not treated properly, they may become unfixable, which can end an athlete's career. Treatment for most overuse injuries starts with the R.I.C.E. method—Rest, Ice, Compression (with an elastic bandage), and Elevation. These treatments allow time for recovery and decrease pain, swelling, and inflammation. Pain medications and drugs that decrease inflammation may also be used. In some cases, surgery may be necessary to repair a damaged tendon or ligament.

Overuse Injuries in Baseball

The most common overuse injuries in baseball are related to overhand throwing and especially affect the shoulder and elbow. "Throwing a baseball is one of the fastest and most violent maneuvers that any joint in the body is subjected to," says Dr. Shane Seroyer, sports medicine physician at Rush University Medical Center in Chicago, Illinois. "The violent

Careers in Sports Medicine

Sports medicine is a very broad field of health care that includes many different professionals, from athletic trainers and group exercise instructors to nutritionists and physical therapists to sports medicine physicians, researchers, and psychologists. Sports medicine is mainly concerned with the prevention, diagnosis, and treatment of sports-related injuries to the muscles, bones, and joints, but sports medicine professionals may also focus on nutrition, psychology, rehabilitation after injury, or maximizing athletic performance. Sports medicine used to be confined to the care of college, professional, and Olympic athletes by a team doctor, but it has evolved to include care of other people such as amateur athletes, dancers, older people, children in youth sports, and regular folks who want to stay physically healthy and maximize their quality of life.

Education for a career in sports medicine depends on the area of interest. Almost all careers in sports medicine require at least a college degree. For example, an athletic trainer, who works directly with athletes at the high school, college, or professional level, earns a degree from an accredited athletic training program and then takes a national examination to get certified as an athletic trainer. Some careers, such as strength and conditioning coaching, require a Master's Degree after college as well as a certification exam. Those who wish to work in sports science research, usually done in hospitals or universities, need an advanced degree such as a PhD. Sports medicine physicians go to medical school after college and then specialize in a related field, such as orthopedics, during their residency, another three to five years. Most physicians also do a fellowship of one to two years of focused sports medicine practice.

and rapid motion places numerous structures in the shoulder at risk for injury."[10]

Pitchers are particularly susceptible to throwing injuries because they may throw as many as one hundred pitches or more in a game. For this reason young pitchers up to the age of seventeen, whose bones and joints have not stopped growing, are monitored closely to make sure they do not throw pitches that can cause serious damage in the future. According to Dr. Seroyer, shoulder injuries from throwing most often come from one of five causes—damaged cartilage, rotator cuff tears, damage to tissues around the shoulder blade, impingement, or neurovascular problems.

The cartilage that surrounds and cushions the shoulder joint is called the "labrum." The labrum holds the head of the humerus (the long bone in the upper arm) in place in the socket of the shoulder joint. Tears in the labrum are among the most common shoulder injuries in baseball. As cartilage wears down with age and overuse, tears become more likely. Another common injury occurs to the rotator cuff. The rotator cuff is the name given to a group of muscles and tendons in the shoulder that stabilize the shoulder. Overuse of the rotator cuff can cause tears in the muscles and inflammation of the tendons, a condition called "tendonitis" or "pitcher's shoulder." Rotator cuff injury can cause pain that goes down into the elbow and may weaken the arm (dead-arm syndrome) and decrease throwing velocity. Proper conditioning and throwing technique are very important because treatment of rotator cuff injuries can be difficult.

Pain around the area of the shoulder blade, or scapula, while throwing is most often a result of inadequate conditioning and poor throwing technique, causing the scapula to move in an abnormal way. This kind of injury can also lead to dead-arm syndrome. Related to scapula pain is impingement. Impingement means that the scapula is putting pressure on the rotator cuff. Impingement can cause swelling and pain in front of the shoulder and makes lifting the arm difficult. Neurovascular disorders are another kind of impingement injury caused by overuse. They are more uncommon than other overuse injuries, but they can cause major damage. They happen when nerves or blood vessels are impinged upon by swelling or damaged tissue as they travel through a joint such as the shoulder, elbow, or wrist. The athlete may feel weakness, pain, numbness, or tingling in the arm and hand. As many as one-third of athletes who develop a neurovascular problem will need surgery to release the pressure on the nerve or blood vessel.

Overuse Injury of the Elbow

Athletes who are prone to rotator cuff injuries because of improper throwing technique are also at risk for overuse injuries to the elbow. Frequent, repetitive, hard throwing puts a great deal of strain on the elbow as well as the shoulder. One elbow injury that can be especially damaging is a tear to the ulnar collateral ligament, or UCL, a ligament in the elbow. The UCL runs along the inner side of the elbow and, along with the radial collateral ligament, or RCL, on the outside of the elbow, stabilizes the elbow and prevents it from moving too much from side to side. Research stud-

Arthroscopic Surgery

Arthroscopic surgery, or arthroscopy, is a surgical procedure in which the inside of a joint is examined and sometimes treated using an arthroscope, a miniature (about pencil-sized) telescope that is inserted into the joint through a small incision about a quarter of an inch long. The surgeon attaches the arthroscope to a camera and a light-carrying cord, which are connected to a video monitor, to see the inside of the joint. The surgeon can also take pictures of the joint with the camera.

Arthroscopy can be done to evaluate an injury or to treat injuries, such as torn cartilage or ligaments. The procedure can be used in many joints, including the shoulder, elbow, wrist, knee, ankle, and hip. An advantage of arthroscopy is that the joint does not have to be opened up with a large incision. Instead, only two small incisions are made—one for the arthroscope and one for other surgical instruments used for repairing the injury. This reduces pain after surgery, causes less trauma to the surrounding tissue, and decreases recovery time. It also helps reduce scarring so that the repaired joint functions better. Athletes who have arthroscopic surgery on their knees, for example, can usually be up walking on crutches the next day.

Arthroscopy has been around since the 1920s, but it was used mainly to diagnose problems that were then fixed with a traditional larger incision. In the 1950s doctors developed the ability to treat injuries with the arthroscope, but operations were risky because the light bulb in the scope could shatter inside the joint. The development of cold-light fiberoptics in the 1970s made arthroscopy safer and more reliable. Today, arthroscopic surgery is the most often performed orthopedic procedure in the United States.

ies have shown that the biggest risk factor for UCL damage is the number of pitches thrown, rather than the type of pitches or the style of throwing. Throwing breaking balls

TOMMY JOHN SURGERY

Tommy John Surgery is used to repair the ulnar collateral ligament (UCL), a tendon that stabilizes the elbow joint during movement.

Ulna

Humerus

During the procedure, a surgeon drills tunnels into the humerus and ulna bones.

She uses tendon removed from the patient's opposite forearm or hamstring to weave a figure eight pattern through the holes. The borrowed tendon replaces the damaged UCL and restores stability to the elbow joint.

such as sliders, however, has been shown to increase risk for such injuries.

Until 1974 damage to the UCL meant the end of a pitcher's career. In that year a pitcher for the Los Angeles Dodgers named Tommy John became the first professional athlete to undergo surgery to repair his UCL, and the procedure became known as "Tommy John" surgery. In this procedure, a tendon is taken from the opposite forearm or from below the knee to replace the damaged UCL. As the procedure has improved over the years, the chances for full recovery have reached about 85 to 90 percent. Tommy John returned to the major leagues after his surgery and was able to pitch until he was forty-six years old.

Acute Traumatic Injuries in Baseball

Unlike overuse injuries, which develop over time and with repeated use, acute injuries happen suddenly, usually as a result of a hard impact or from a sudden, abnormal movement of a body part. Some common acute injuries for which baseball players are at risk are fractures, sprains and strains, and torn cartilage or ligaments in the knee.

In October 1914 *The New York Times* reported that "Red Smith, the third baseman of the champions [the Boston Braves], broke his right leg just above the ankle while sliding to second base in the ninth inning of the first game of the double-header. The break was a severe one and it will be a long time before Smith is able to walk. It is doubtful if the Braves' third baseman will ever be able to play ball again."[11] Sliding into a base is the most common cause of bone fractures in baseball. If the cleats catch on the base, but the body keeps moving forward, the bones in the lower leg, the tibia and the fibula, can snap near the ankle. Another cause of broken bones in baseball is being hit by a pitched or batted baseball, especially in an area where little muscle tissue covers the bone. In July 1967 St. Louis Cardinals pitcher Bob Gibson was hit squarely on the right leg just above the ankle by a hard line drive off the bat of Roberto Clemente. The impact was enough to break the fibula, the smaller of the two lower leg bones.

Fortunately, the chances for full recovery from a broken leg are much better now than they were in 1914, and fractures need not end a player's career. Most leg and ankle fractures are surgically treated with special screws and plates that hold the bones together while they heal. One good thing about bones is that, unlike soft tissues, which form weakened scar tissue as they heal, bones heal with just as much strength as they had before the fracture. With proper management and enough time allowed for healing, baseball players can come back from most fractures with no loss of ability. Bob Gibson came back to the Cardinals after two months out and pitched three winning games in the World Series. In March 1997 White Sox third baseman Robin Ventura broke his ankle sliding into home. After he came back in July, he reached base safely in twenty-one games in a row.

Los Angeles Dodgers pitcher Tommy John, seen here, became the first professional athlete to undergo surgery to repair his UCL. The procedure, which became known as "Tommy John" surgery is now commonly performed by doctors.

Other fractures in baseball include fractured fingers and hands from being hit by a pitch or by catching a ball with the bare hand instead of a gloved hand. These are treated with a splint or cast to immobilize the bone and allow it to heal. Bones in the face can be broken from a collision with another player or by being hit with a pitched ball. These fractures may require surgery to line up the broken bones and fix them with tiny metal plates and screws. Less common is "ball thrower's fracture," which refers to a spiral-shaped fracture of the humerus, the bone of the upper arm, caused by extreme muscle contraction and intense torsion, or twisting, from throwing the ball improperly and too forcefully. This fracture is more common in inexperienced and younger players, and is treated with a cast followed by a brace until the bone is healed.

Sprains and Strains

Sprains and strains are very common in baseball. A sprain is an injury of a ligament, the tough, fibrous bands that holds the bones together at a joint. They support the skeleton and prevent joints from moving in abnormal directions. If the joint is suddenly moved in an abnormal way, the ligament can be overstretched or torn, which makes the joint unstable. Symptoms of a sprain include sharp pain in the joint, swelling, and bruising.

Sprains commonly occur to the knee or ankle, when the athlete steps on an uneven surface (such as a base or another player's foot) and turns the foot or the knee sideways. This overstretches the ligaments along the outer surface of the ankle. Sliding head first into a base can cause a wrist sprain. Sprains are classified by their severity as Grade I, II, or III. Grades I and II can usually be treated with the R.I.C.E. method. Prompt treatment can help a sprained joint recover in a few days. If treatment is delayed, recovery can take weeks. Grade III sprains can leave the athlete with permanent joint instability, and surgery may be necessary, followed by physical therapy.

A strain is similar to a sprain except that it affects a muscle or a tendon. Strains are caused by overstretching or tearing of the muscle or tendon. They are also classified as Grade I, II, or III, depending on severity. Grade I strains are commonly called "pulled" muscles. Grade II involves more tearing of the muscle tissue, but the muscle can still contract. Grade III strains involve complete rupture, or a breaking open, of the muscle, and the muscle cannot contract at all. Symptoms of a strain include sudden, sharp pain in the muscle and difficulty using the body part affected. Grade III tears also include a visible deformity in the torn muscle and bleeding into the muscle.

Lower grade muscle strains are most often treated with pain medicines such as ibuprofen or Tylenol and the R.I.C.E. method, followed by a program of gentle stretching and strengthening. They are usually better after two to three days. More severe strains may require surgery to repair the tear and may take several weeks to recover.

Baseball players commonly strain a hamstring, the large muscle in the back of the thigh, when they start running suddenly to get out of the batter's box after a hit or to steal a base. Both sprains and strains can be avoided by keeping the muscles and joints flexible, properly warming up before exercise and stretching afterwards, not trying to do too much too soon, and by wearing proper footwear for the sport.

Injuries to the Knee

Traumatic knee injuries are very common in many sports, including baseball. Knee injuries usually involve a tear to the ligaments or cartilage in the knee. Cartilage in the knee is called the "meniscus." There are two of them—the lateral meniscus on the outside and the medial meniscus on the inside. These C-shaped pieces of cartilage act as cushions between the femur (thighbone) and the tibia (shinbone). A meniscus can get torn when the knee is forcefully rotated or twisted while the foot is planted on the ground. Baseball players can tear their meniscus when making a sharp turn around the bases, by changing direction suddenly in the field, or by colliding with another player.

Symptoms of a torn meniscus include pain, especially when the knee is straightened, and swelling. There may be a

Knee Anatomy

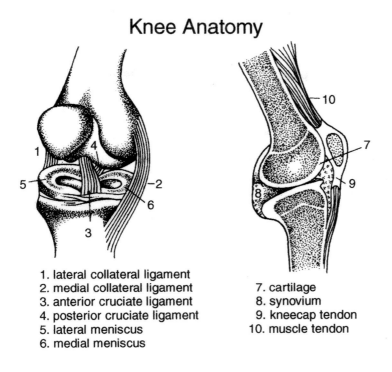

1. lateral collateral ligament
2. medial collateral ligament
3. anterior cruciate ligament
4. posterior cruciate ligament
5. lateral meniscus
6. medial meniscus

7. cartilage
8. synovium
9. kneecap tendon
10. muscle tendon

An illustration showing the anatomy of the knee. Injuries to the knee are very common in various sports, including baseball.

clicking or popping sound when the player flexes the knee. A fragment of torn meniscus can get caught between the femur and the tibia and cause the knee to lock. Minor tears can be treated with rest and muscle-strengthening exercises. More severe tears, or minor tears that have become worse over time, may need surgery to remove the torn pieces of cartilage. A period of physical therapy follows surgery until the injury is healed.

The anterior cruciate ligament, or ACL, and the posterior cruciate ligament, the PCL, are the two major ligaments in the knee that hold the femur and the tibia together and stabilize the joint. "Anterior" means "front," "posterior" means "back," and "cruciate" means "shaped like a cross." The ACL crosses in front of the PCL like an "X" so that the knee can move forward or backward but not sideways. If the knee is forcefully pushed sideways or twisted, the ACL or PCL can tear. ACL injuries most often happen from sudden changes in direction, abrupt stopping, or landing badly after jumping. The PCL is most commonly injured from a sudden impact to the front of the knee.

Injuries to the cruciate ligaments may not always cause immediate pain, but there may be a loud popping sound as the ligament is torn away from the bone. Treatment depends on the severity of the injury and may range from the R.I.C.E. method, anti-inflammatory pain medications, and physical therapy for partial tears to surgery to replace a completely torn ligament.

Baseball Injuries in Children

Because children are not fully mature physically, mentally, or emotionally, they are especially prone to certain injuries when playing baseball. Their muscles, tendons, ligaments, and joints are not developed fully, so children are prone to sprains and strains from trying to do too much, especially if they are trying to please their coaches or their parents watching from the stands. Children lack the physical coordination of the more experienced adult, so they have less control of their bodies. Also, they may not have a complete understanding of how to move on the playing field, so collisions with other players are common, leading to broken bones and concussions. Young pitchers do not have complete command of their pitches yet, so batters are at risk of getting hit with the ball and suffering bruises, cracked teeth, broken noses, or black eyes.

Young pitchers have their own set of injuries that their coaches can help guard against. Pitchers are often pressured to throw more complex, advanced pitches at a young age. Coaches can limit the type and number of pitches thrown, depending on the age and skill level of the pitcher. Dr. Charles Bush-Joseph, sports medicine specialist at Rush University Hospital in Chicago, says, "For pitchers under fourteen years old, we encourage fast ball and change-up [lower velocity] pitches and discourage the use of a curveball to prevent injury."[12] He recommends that pitchers under ten throw no more than fifty pitches

BATTER'S BOX

1.5 million

The number of kids treated in emergency rooms for baseball injuries from 1994 to 2006. Almost half of the injuries were caused by being hit in the face.

per game and seventy-five per week, and that they not throw sliders until they are at least seventeen. Breaking pitches such as curves and sliders require more movement of the arm and place more stress on the shoulder and elbow. Painful overuse injuries such as "pitcher's elbow" (tiny tears in the tendons and ligaments in the elbow) and "little leaguer's shoulder" (which is actually a fracture of the top of the humerus) can result in a player having to miss as much as three months of the baseball season. Most injuries of this type are treated with plenty of rest for the injured joint, followed by gradual return to the game.

Children are especially prone to injuries while playing baseball because they have not yet matured physically, mentally, or emotionally to meet some of the more challenging aspects of the game.

CHAPTER 4

Curves, Sliders, and Knuckleballs— The Science of Pitching

Hall of Fame pitcher Warren Spahn once said, "Hitting is timing. Pitching is upsetting timing."[13] Many sports fans might say that there is no greater battle in sports than that between a pitcher on the mound and the batter standing at the plate. The battle is a silent one, but no less intense for its silence. Each one staring the other one down, the batter trying to second guess the pitcher and predict what kind of pitch will be thrown; the pitcher choosing the perfect pitch for this particular batter that will get the desired results—a pop fly, a strike-out, or an easy grounder for a double play. In this classic battle, the pitcher usually wins. Pitchers know what they are going to throw; batters have to guess.

Although the spectators can not see it, a great deal of strategy goes into each pitch, depending on the particular situation—the score, the inning, the batter's skill, how many men are on base and which bases they are on, how many balls and strikes have already been thrown, and many more factors. A pitcher has many options when it comes to choosing his pitch, and a good pitcher is skilled at several of them. Each kind of pitch has its purpose and requires its

The Evolution of the Baseball

Early baseballs were handmade, so their size and weight varied according to how and where they were made. Most baseballs started with a core of either cork or rubber wound with yarn or string and wrapped with a leather cover stitched in place. By the time baseball became professional in the late 1800s, the manufacture of baseballs became more standardized. The core was made of rubber, but the string was still wound around it by hand, so balls were not uniform in shape and weight.

In 1909 the core was changed to cork covered with a thin layer of rubber. A cork core is somewhat springier than pure rubber, and these balls bounced off the bat better. In the 1920s hand-winding the string was replaced with machine-winding, which allowed for a much tighter, denser ball, and made the ball even livelier off the bat. During World War II, a shortage of rubber led to a temporary change to balata, a material similar to rubber but not as bouncy. Balata deadened the ball, so the number of home runs hit and runs scored declined during that time.

The rubber-wrapped cork core returned in 1945, and baseballs have not changed since then. Major league rules are very specific about the composition, size, and weight of today's baseballs. A ball can be no larger than 9 1/4 inches (23.5cm) around and weigh no more than 5 ounces (142g).

A regulation baseball cut in half to show its interior. The center contains cork that is covered by rubber that is then covered by cotton and wool yarn.

own special delivery from the pitcher. Pitchers understand the science, especially the physics, behind pitching—the factors that affect how the baseball will travel through the air. Physicist Linda Shore of the San Francisco Exploratorium says, "There's a lot of physics in baseball. When I was a kid, I loved baseball but all I wanted to see was hitting, hitting, hitting. Once I understood the physics of pitching, it became so much more interesting."[14]

The Windup

The various physical forces that affect how a pitch moves through the air begin with the pitcher himself, and it all starts with two basic biomechanical principles: conservation of momentum and sequential summation of movement.

The law of conservation of momentum states that momentum created in a moving object remains the same (it is conserved) even when that momentum is transferred to another object. In physics, "momentum" means how much motion an object has. The amount of momentum a moving object has depends on two things—its mass and its velocity. In mathematical terms, momentum (expressed as "p," thought to come from the Latin word "petere," meaning "to go forward.") is equal to mass (m) times velocity (v), or

$$p = mv$$

Mass is not quite the same as weight. Weight depends on gravity; mass does not. Mass is a measure of how much matter an object contains. A bowling ball weighs much less on the moon than it does on the Earth because the moon has much less gravitational pull on the bowling ball than the Earth does, but the ball's mass is the same on the moon as it is on the Earth. The more mass an object has, the more force it takes to make it change direction or speed when it is moving. If a person has a pound of Styrofoam and a pound of granite, it takes less force to push the Styrofoam because it has less mass than the granite.

The other force affecting momentum is velocity, or how fast an object is changing its original position. Just as mass is not the same as weight, velocity is not the same as speed.

MOMENTUM IN THE PITCH

The law of conservation of momentum states that momentum created in a moving object remains the same even when that momentum is transferred to another object. In pitching a baseball, momentum is created and transferred through the pitcher's body movements. When this momentum is transferred from a larger object (the pitcher) to a smaller one (the baseball), it will cause the smaller object to move faster than the larger object that gave the momentum.

1 When a pitcher prepares to pitch, he leans his weight back on one foot and raises his front leg. Momentum is being built up in the large muscles of the lower body.

2 As he moves forward, he lunges the front leg forward and brings his pitching arm back, building more momentum in his lower body and additional momentum in his arm.

3 As he plants his front foot, his lower body stops its forward motion, and the built-up momentum is transferred from his lower body to his torso, which bends forward.

4 As his upper body and his throwing arm move forward, the momentum is transferred from the upper body to the arm, then to the wrist, which snaps like the end of a whip as the hand and fingers finally propel the ball forward. Adding to the momentum is the rotational movement of the pitcher's body around his planted foot and the step downhill from the pitcher's mound.

Speed measures how fast an object is moving—how much distance it covers in a certain length of time. Velocity adds direction to speed. For example, a person running on a treadmill may be running at a speed of 8 miles (12.74m) per hour, but the runner is not moving in any direction, so the velocity is zero.

The second principle, sequential summation of movement, means that if the conserved momentum is transferred from a larger object to a smaller one, it will cause the smaller object to move faster than the larger object that provided the momentum. For example, when a person cracks a whip, momentum builds up in the person's body and is then transferred through the arm, hand, and wrist, then through the whip until it reaches the tip. By that point the tip is moving so fast that it actually breaks the sound barrier. The "crack" of the whip is actually a mini sonic boom!

When pitchers prepare to pitch, they lean their weight back on one foot and raise their front leg. Momentum builds up in the large muscles of the lower body. As the pitchers move forward, they lunge their front legs forward and bring their pitching arms back, building more momentum in their lower bodies and additional momentum in their arms. As they plant their front feet, their lower bodies stop their forward motion, and the built-up momentum is transferred from their lower bodies to their torsos, which bend forward. As their upper bodies and their throwing arms move forward, the momentum is transferred from their upper bodies to their arms, then to their wrists, which snap like the end of a whip as the hands and fingers finally propel the ball forward. All this momentum, transferred from the large lower body to the much smaller baseball, is expressed in the blistering speed of the ball as it leaves the pitcher's hand.

Adding to this is the rotational movement of the pitcher's body around the planted foot. It is similar to a ball being whirled around at the end of a string. The longer the string, the more momentum the ball has and the faster it will move through the air if it is released from the string. This is why taller pitchers tend to be able to throw faster than shorter ones. One more factor is the height of the pitcher's mound. The standard mound is 10 inches (25.4cm) high. The fact that the pitcher is stepping downhill to release the ball adds to the momentum built into the pitch, thereby adding velocity to the throw.

The Delivery

Velocity alone does not make a good pitcher. An effective pitcher must be able to fool the batter with a variety of pitches. Since baseball's beginnings, pitchers have invented

The delivery of the ball is important in baseball. A good pitcher must be able to fool the batter with a variety of pitches.

more than a dozen different kinds of pitches. Each one moves through the air in its own way on its flight to the plate, depending not only on its velocity but also on what spin the pitcher puts on the ball as it is released. Pitchers can vary the way the ball spins by the way they grip the ball and by the way they snap their wrists as they release it. The reason that different spins make the ball move in different ways in the air is because of the Magnus force, also called the Magnus effect.

The Magnus force is named after the German scientist Gustav Magnus, who demonstrated in 1852 that a spinning object will change its path, or trajectory, as it moves through the air, depending on the direction of the spin. As a ball moves forward through the air, the flow of air is deflected around the ball. If the ball is not spinning at all, the pressure of the air moving around it is equal on all sides, and the ball's trajectory does not change.

When the ball is spinning forward as it moves, the pitcher is said to have topspin on it. When this happens, another principle of physics, Bernoulli's principle, comes into play. First introduced by Swiss mathematician Daniel Bernoulli in the eighteenth century, Bernoulli's principle says that the faster air moves over the surface of an object, the less pressure the air puts on the object. When a ball has topspin on it, the top of the ball is moving in the opposite direction from the flow of the air (relative to the direction of the ball), but the bottom of the ball is moving in the same direction as the flow of the air. This creates more air resistance, or drag, on the top of the ball and less on the bottom. The drag makes the air move slower over the top of the ball and faster under the bottom. The slower-moving air over the top exerts more pressure on the ball than the faster moving air under the ball. This creates the Magnus force, which forces the ball to move downward as it moves forward. This is how a curveball is thrown.

Gustav Magnus

Gustav Magnus was a German chemist and physicist. He was born May 2, 1802, in Berlin, Germany. His father was wealthy, and Gustav was able to attend the best schools in Berlin. After finishing his education in Berlin, he went to Stockholm, Sweden, and studied with Jakob Berzelius, a Swedish chemist who, along with several others, is known as a father of modern chemistry. Later Magnus went to Paris, France, and worked with Joseph Louis Gay-Lussac and Louis Jacques Thénard, both Frenchmen who made important contributions to chemistry and physics. In 1831 Magnus returned to Berlin and became a professor at the university there.

Magnus was very successful and well respected as a professor. He was able to explain complicated chemical and physical concepts clearly and spent a great deal of time with his students, taking them to factories around the city to show them examples of those concepts. He also had students come to his own home every week for discussions about chemistry and physics.

In his own research, he studied a wide variety of topics, including how gases are absorbed in blood and how heat expands them, the nature of electricity, and the

Gustav Magnus was a German chemist and physicist who was responsible for describing the Magnus effect, the effect of spin on the flight of an object.

behavior of projectiles fired from guns. This last topic led to his description of the effect of spin on the flight of an object (observations that had actually been made by Isaac Newton almost two hundred years earlier), which came to be known as the Magnus effect. Magnus died in Berlin in 1870.

The opposite happens when backspin is put on the ball. Now the top of the ball is moving in the same direction as the airflow, and the bottom of the ball is moving against the airflow. The increased drag and increased pressure on the bottom of the ball means that the Magnus force makes it stay up rather than sink. A fastball thrown this way may even appear to rise at it approaches the plate.

A pitcher can also put some sidespin on the ball. Sidespin is the kind of spin that a toy top has or, on a larger scale, the kind the Earth has as it rotates. A combination of topspin and sidespin makes the ball break slightly to the right or the left as well as down. Most pitchers throw the curve with a diagonal spin so that it moves both down and to the left of a right-hander and down and to the right of a lefty.

Magnus Force and Gravity

Another force that acts on a pitched ball is gravity, the downward pull on an object created by the mass of the Earth. As a 95-mile- (152.89-km-) per-hour fastball approaches the plate, gravity causes it to drop as much as 2 feet (0.61m) from its release point to the plate. A slower pitch, such as a change-up, might drop as much as 5 feet (1.52m), just due to gravity.

The effect of gravity can be seen when a slider is thrown. This pitch has a lateral, or sideways, spin similar to that of a bullet or a football. Because of this direction of spin, Magnus forces have less effect on a slider as long as it moves in a straight line. When gravity starts to pull it down, however, the direction of spin changes in relation to the path of the ball. The trajectory of the slider bends, so the ball "breaks" sideways and downward. A slider breaks right to left when thrown by a right-handed pitcher and left to right from a left-handed pitcher. A screwball is like a slider, but it moves the opposite way. Delivering a screwball is difficult because of the spin necessary to make it break the way it does, so few pitchers throw it.

Magnus Forces and the Ball Surface

Magnus forces are even more significant when the ball has a rough surface, which a baseball has because of the stitched seams on it. There is more drag over the seams than there is over the smooth parts of the ball, so the ball's movement

Pitchers may apply substances, such pine tar, to a baseball to make it sticky, easier to grip, and create more spin. The use of such materials is illegal and can get professional league pitchers fined or even suspended.

varies depending on how the seams are spinning and how they are interacting with the air. In a two-seam fastball, for example, the pitcher grips the ball with his index and middle fingers lying along two lines of stitches. For a four-seam fastball, the grip is such that his index and middle fingers are lying across the lines of stitches at their widest part. By changing the grip this way, the seams spin differently when the ball is thrown, and so the ball behaves differently. Many pitchers believe that the four-seam fastball breaks more than the two-seam pitch because of the increased interaction of the seams with the air, creating more of a Magnus effect.

The low-velocity knuckleball has almost no spin at all; it rotates only once on its way to the batter. The slow rotation moves the seams around, which changes the direction of the drag on the ball and allows the ball to be pushed in several directions before it reaches the plate. This makes its motion very unpredictable for the batter (as well as for the catcher trying to catch it).

Throughout the history of baseball, pitchers have attempted to confuse batters by altering the surface of the baseball to change Magnus forces and make the ball do unpredictable things in flight. They have scuffed the ball with nail files or other objects to increase the drag on one side. In 1987 Minnesota Twins pitcher Joe Niekro was caught with a nail file and a piece of sandpaper that he had used to scuff the ball. In 1980 Seattle Mariners pitcher Rick Honeycutt taped a thumbtack to his finger to cut the surface of the ball. Pitchers have applied substances such as saliva, hair grease, or tobacco juice to the ball to make it slip more easily out of the fingers. Hall of Fame pitcher Gaylord Perry was suspended for coating the ball with so much Vaseline that his catcher could not throw it back to him. Other pitchers have applied substances such as pine tar to make the ball sticky, which they believed would give them a better grip on the ball and create more spin. Altering the surface of a baseball is illegal, and can get a pitcher suspended or fined.

CHAPTER 5

"Swing and a Long One!"—When the Bat Meets the Ball

Hall-of-Famer Yogi Berra is quoted as asking, "How can you hit and think at the same time?"[15] It sounds humorous, but it really is a very good question. It has been suggested that the most difficult skill in all of sports is to hit a round ball with a round bat, and it is made even more complicated by the skill of the pitcher. A batter standing at home plate has about one-quarter of a second to make a judgment about the speed and direction of a 3-inch- (7.62-cm-) wide ball hurtling at 90 miles (144.84km) per hour from the pitcher's mound only 60 feet (18.23m), 6 inches (15.24cm) away. Then batters still have to make the decision about whether or not to swing at the ball and, if they decide to swing, where and when to swing the bat to make good contact with the ball.

Because the skill of hitting a baseball is so difficult, baseball is the only sport in which a player can succeed only one-third of the time (a .333 batting average) and still be considered good enough to earn an excellent living and get into the Hall of Fame. Making solid contact with the baseball requires focused concentration, superb eyesight, quick reaction time, good body mechanics, power, and lots and lots of practice. Even when good contact is made, forces such as spin, gravity, and air resistance all affect how the ball will travel after it is hit.

Seeing the Pitch

Children learning to play baseball are frequently told, "Keep your eye on the ball." That advice works fine at lower levels of play when the ball is coming toward the plate at a relatively slow velocity. At the major league level, however, that advice is of little help because the human eye is not capable of remaining focused on a baseball moving at 90 miles (144.84km) per hour. Ken Fuld, professor of psychology at the University of New Hampshire, says that it is physically impossible for a hitter to keep his eye on the ball all the way to the plate. "Good hitters fixate on a pitcher's release point," he says, "and then make an eye movement (called an eye saccade) to track the ball (called a smooth pursuit eye movement) for as long as possible. A good hitter can track the ball to within about 5 feet (1.52m); a not-so-good hitter loses eye contact at about ten feet."[16]

According to Yale professor Dr. Robert Adair, author of *The Physics of Baseball*, once the ball leaves the pitcher's hand, it takes about a tenth of a second (0.1 seconds) for the batter's eye to see the ball and send the information to the brain. The brain needs another .075 seconds to process this information and decide the location and velocity of the pitch. In that time, 0.175 seconds (less than one-fifth of a second), the ball has already traveled 14 of its 60 feet (18.23m), 6 inches (15.24cm) to the plate. The batter now has about 0.125 seconds to decide when and where to swing. By then the ball is only 25 feet (7.62m) away. The swing itself lasts about 0.150 seconds, and at that point the ball has arrived. A batter who decides at the last instant not to swing must react within the first 0.05 (five one-hundredths) second of the swing to pull the bat back. It is not fully understood how a human being can predict where a fast-moving ball will be when it arrives, but some clues, however, help the batter "see" the pitch and so know what to expect from it.

First is the angle of the pitcher's arm as the pitch is delivered. An overhand delivery may indicate a pitch with more backspin, whereas a more sidearm delivery might indicate sidespin on the ball. Another clue is how soon or late in the delivery the pitcher releases the ball, and at what angle the ball is leaving his hand. For example, a fastball is released with a slightly downward angle, whereas a slow change-up is delivered with a slightly more upward angle before gravity pulls it down on its way to the plate.

Another clue is how the pitcher is holding the ball. Different grips are used to produce different pitches, and a good batter can see the grip and judge the pitch as it is released. Another effective skill for a batter to have is the ability to judge what spin the ball has on it as it approaches.

A pitcher with a more overhand delivery, like this one, indicates to a batter that the ball will have more backspin on it.

Altering the Bat

Just as pitchers have been known to alter the surface of the ball to give them an advantage, batters have also been known to alter the bat to give them an edge. One way they have done this is by using a "corked" bat. A corked bat is a bat that has been hollowed out and filled with another substance such as cork or small rubber balls. The hole is usually about 1 inch (2.54cm) in diameter and about 10 inches (25.4cm) long.

A corked bat might help a batter because it is lighter by about 1 or 2 ounces. Also, because the lighter material is out near the barrel end of the bat, the balance point of the bat is shifted closer to the batter's hands. Both of these changes help the batter get a faster bat speed during swing, which allows more time to react to the pitch and make a decision about swinging. The lighter weight also gives more control over the swing.

One possible disadvantage to using a corked bat is that the part of the bat that contacts the ball has less mass than a solid wood bat. This cancels out some of the advantage of the faster bat speed. Also corked bats have not been proven to increase the chances of hitting a home run. In fact, research has demonstrated that there is little or no real advantage to using a corked bat. Another consideration is that, like altering the ball, corking the bat is also illegal, and batters who are caught will be suspended or fined.

Depending on the spin, the red seams on the white ball create different images as the ball rotates because of the way the seams pass in front of the batter's view. For example, a four-seam slider appears to the batter to have a red dot on the upper right part of the ball as it spins, but a two-seam slider appears to be solid white at the top. This skill of seeing a pitch and reacting to it requires excellent dynamic visual acuity (the ability to see and interpret moving objects). Even with years of practice, the batter still misses most of the time.

The Swing

Just as in pitching, body mechanics (how the batter uses his body to generate the maximum amount of force on the ball) plays an important role in hitting. The batter stands at the plate with knees bent and hands back, like a tightly coiled

The momentum built up in this batter's body is transferred to the smaller bat he is holding which generates a very fast bat speed and a lot of kinetic energy. This allows the young player to send the ball flying.

spring, ready to swing. As batters swing, they bring the bat around and turn their upper bodies, using rotation to add energy just as the pitcher does. Batters may take a step forward to shift their weight forward and add some momentum to the swing, but they keep their back foot planted firmly on the ground so that all the energy generated in the swing stays in their upper body and arms. The momentum built up in the batter's body is transferred to the smaller bat, which generates a fast bat speed and a lot of kinetic energy.

Isaac Newton's Three Laws of Motion

Isaac Newton (1643–1727) was a renowned mathematician and scientist who, while still in college, developed theories about the physics of motion, light, and gravity. For his work, he was knighted by Queen Anne in 1705. His three laws of motion are:

Law I: An object at rest tends to stay at rest, and an object in motion tends to stay in motion at the same speed and in the same direction, unless acted upon by an unbalanced force. If you push on both sides of a ball, the ball does not move because the force is balanced. If you push on just one side, the ball will roll because the force is unbalanced. Another example is that passengers in a moving car continue to move forward when the car stops suddenly, until stopped by their seatbelt.

Law II: The greater the mass of an object, the greater the force needed to move the object. Heavier objects need more force than lighter objects to make them move. This can be expressed in the mathematical equation Force = mass times acceleration, or $F = ma$. If you know the weight (mass) of an object and how fast it is moving (acceleration), you can figure out how much force is being applied to it. Force is measured in units called "Newtons."

Law III: For every action, there is an opposite and equal reaction. This means that when an object pushes another object, it gets pushed back in the opposite direction with equal force. For example, when a fish pushes water backwards with its fins, the water pushes the fish forward with equal force, which makes it possible for the fish to swim.

Kinetic energy is the energy created by a moving object. When an object with kinetic energy in it hits another object, the kinetic energy is transferred to the hit object, which makes it move also. The faster the object is moving, the more kinetic energy it has, and the faster the hit object will move when it is hit. An object with more mass also imparts more energy than a lighter one. These laws of nature were closely observed and written about in the seventeenth century by English scientist Isaac Newton, best known for his work with gravity and motion.

Baseball and Isaac Newton

Isaac Newton was an English philosopher and physicist who, among many other accomplishments, devised three laws of motion. The second and third of these laws are the most relevant to baseball. Newton's third law of motion says that for every action, there is an opposite and equal reaction. This means that an object that is pushed against pushes back with an equal force, but in the opposite direction. For example, when a frog jumps off a lily pad, both of them exert a force on each other. The frog moves forward, and the lily pad moves backward.

Both the baseball and the bat exert force on each other when they make contact. The reason that the bat moves the ball but the ball does not move the bat has to do with Newton's second law of motion, which says that the object with the greater mass or greater speed puts more force on the object with less mass or less speed. Newton's second law can

English philosopher and physicist Isaac Newton devised the three laws of motion, which play a major role in baseball.

be expressed in an equation similar to the one used to express conservation of momentum: Force (F) is equal to mass (m) times acceleration (a), or

$$F = ma$$

If the mass of an object is increased, the force it exerts is greater than the force exerted by the object with less mass. Bat speed and pitch speed are often close to equal, so since the mass of the bat is greater than the mass of the ball, more force is put on the ball than on the bat, and the ball is sent flying. A batter can also send a ball farther by using a larger bat (with more mass), as long as the batter has enough power to maintain the same bat speed.

A fast swing and a heavy bat are only part of hitting a ball far, however, because the ball is also moving at a high velocity. The kinetic energy transferred from the bat to the ball provides some of the energy that sends the ball flying, but not all of it. There is also kinetic energy in the ball. When both objects involved in a collision are moving instead of just one, the resulting reaction is greater. This why a bunted ball does not go very far; the bat moves very little in a bunt. A fast swing, along with a fast pitch, creates more kinetic energy than it would with a slower pitch. The ball comes off the bat faster, and the more velocity the ball has off the bat, the farther it will go.

Making Contact—The Trampoline Effect

Another factor that affects how the ball comes off the bat is elasticity. Whenever two objects collide, the surface of both objects is dented or compressed to some degree as long as the objects are not absolutely rigid. The faster the object resumes its original shape, the more elasticity it has. For example, if a person pushes his finger against an inflated balloon, the balloon bounces back to its original shape as soon as the finger is removed. Balloons have a lot of elasticity. If the person presses his finger into a ball of clay, the hole it makes stays there. The clay does not return to its original shape because clay has almost no elasticity.

Even though a bat is made of wood or metal and a baseball seems to be very hard, both of them have some elasticity. Ultra-slow motion photography shows that when the bat makes contact with the ball, both surfaces are compressed to some degree, but they both spring back to their original shape within a few thousandths of a second. During the collision, some of the kinetic energy is converted into heat, caused by the friction of the two surfaces contacting each other. The faster the ball and bat bounce back to their original shape, however, the less kinetic energy is lost as heat, and the more energy is conserved as motion. Elasticity helps to conserve kinetic energy. This is sometimes called the "trampoline effect." When a person jumps on a trampoline, most of the kinetic energy of the jump is conserved because the trampoline is elastic and resumes its shape quickly, propelling the person into the air. If both objects have elasticity, such as a baseball and a bat, the rebound, or "trampoline effect," is even greater.

BATTER'S BOX
Timing is Everything!
Swinging the bat even 1/100 of a second too soon or too late will cause the ball to go foul.

Hitting and Spin

The effect of spin on a baseball is as important in hitting as it is in pitching. Spin is a major factor in determining how far a ball will carry after it is hit. Imagine a bat hitting a ball in slow motion. If the bat contacts the ball on its upper half, it will make the ball spin forward. In other words, it will have topspin on it. Just as a pitched ball with topspin tends to drop because of the Magnus effect, a ball hit with topspin will also tend to drop, which usually results in a grounder that hits the ground in front of the plate.

Conversely, if the batter hits the ball on its lower half, the ball will have backspin. Magnus forces will cause the ball with backspin to stay up longer so that it will go farther. Home run hitters not only have power, they also know how to hit a ball with enough backspin to keep it up long enough to carry it right out of the park for a home run. The more a

Spin is just as important in hitting as it is in pitching and is the major factor in determining how far a ball will go after it is hit.

batter "gets under" a ball, however, the more backspin it will have, and the more vertical its trajectory, or flight path, will be. Too much backspin results in a pop fly. Gravity will bring it down to the fielder before it reaches the fence. If the batter really gets under the ball, the ball will go straight up.

If a batter hits the ball squarely in the center, little spin will be put on it. This results in a line drive that only comes down when gravity exerts its effect. A skilled batter can hit a hard line drive with enough topspin to make it land in front of the fielder for a base hit, or enough backspin to make it sail over the fielder's head.

Air Resistance

Good hitters use spin and its effect on air resistance to get a good hit. Air resistance also greatly affects the flight of a ball after it is hit. When a baseball is first hit, the momentum transferred to it and the Magnus forces acting on it are enough to overcome the pull of gravity for a short time. Soon, however, air resistance comes into play to slow the ball down.

MAGNUS FORCE ON A BASEBALL

Scientist Gustav Magnus demonstrated that a spinning object will change its path as it moves through the air, depending on the direction of the spin. As a baseball moves forward through the air, the flow of air is deflected around the ball. If the ball does not spin, it will remain on a straight path. If the ball spins forward, it is said to have topspin and will move downward. If the ball rotates backward, it is said to have backspin and will move upward.

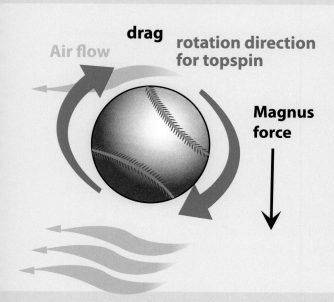

Topspin: The top of the ball moves in the opposite direction from the flow of the air, but the bottom of the ball is moving in the same direction as the flow of the air. This creates more air resistance, or drag, on the top of the ball and less on the bottom. The slower-moving air over the top exerts more pressure on the ball than the faster moving air under the ball. This creates the Magnus force, which forces the ball to move downward as it moves forward.

Backspin: The top of the ball moves in the same direction as the flow of the air, but the bottom of the ball is moving in the opposite direction as the flow of the air. This creates more air resistance, or drag, on the bottom of the ball and less on the top. The slower-moving air over the bottom exerts more pressure on the ball than the faster moving air on top of the ball. This creates the Magnus force, which forces the ball to move upward as it moves forward.

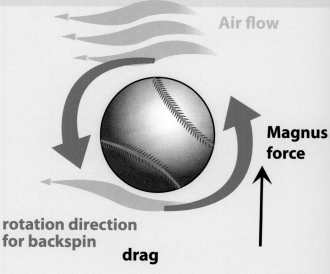

Whenever two objects rub against each other, friction is created. Friction changes kinetic energy into thermal energy, or heat, so some kinetic energy is lost. For example people who feel cold might rub their arms to use friction to warm them. A baseball traveling through the air collides with the molecules of air, causing friction between the air molecules and the ball. Some of the ball's kinetic energy is lost as thermal energy because of the friction.

At higher altitudes air is thinner. It has less density, which means that the air molecules are farther apart than they are at

Fastballs vs. Curves—Which Goes Farther?

Baseball fans love to debate about whether a fastball or a curveball is more likely to be hit for a home run. Most believe that the fastball will go farther because it has more velocity and therefore more kinetic energy. Physicists at the University of California at Davis and the University of Cambridge, England, however, concluded from research they conducted in 2003 that a well-hit curveball has more home run potential, even though it is generally slower than a fastball, because of the spin the curve has on it. As a curveball leaves the pitcher's hand, it has topspin on it; the top of the ball is spinning toward the batter and the bottom of the ball is spinning away from the batter. The batter who hopes to hit a home run wants the ball to have backspin on it when it leaves the bat so it will stay up longer. From the batter's point of view, the curveball already has backspin on it, because the batter's viewpoint is opposite from the pitcher's. For the batter to get backspin, the curveball does not have to change its spin direction.

Conversely, the fastball has backspin from the pitcher's point of view, but has topspin from the batter's point of view. If the batter wants the ball to have the backspin that will provide the needed lift, the ball has to change its direction of spin when it is hit, so energy is lost. For this reason researchers concluded that a well-hit curveball will go farther than a comparably hit fastball.

lower altitudes, so there is less friction between the ball and the air. Professional ballplayers know that it is often easier to hit a home run in Denver, Colorado, than in New York or Miami because the air density in the mountains a mile above sea level is much lower than it is at sea level. When the velocity of the ball has decreased enough because of air resistance, gravity takes over, and the ball heads down toward the ground.

Air interferes with the flight of the ball in several other ways, depending on wind speed and direction, air temperature, and humidity. Wind alters the effect of friction on the ball. If the wind is blowing in the same direction as the ball, less friction is created, and the ball will carry farther than it would have if the air were still. But, if the wind is blowing against the ball, it causes more friction and increases the resistance; thus, a ball that might have been a home run now becomes a long fly ball. Good batters know how to take advantage of wind speed and direction. As Brian Johnson, former San Francisco Giant, says, "Sometimes the wind might be blowing somewhat in towards the plate in left field, and slightly out of the park in right. In that case, [the batter] might take advantage by trying to hit the ball towards right."[17] Candlestick Park in San Francisco, Johnson's former home field, is known for its "jet stream" wind that often blows in from left field toward right field. Left-handed batters who send the ball in that direction can take advantage of that current to send the ball out of the park.

Besides air density and wind speed, the temperature and humidity of the air can affect the flight of the ball. When air is warm, it expands, which means the air molecules become farther apart. Warm air is less dense and exerts less pressure and friction on the ball, so the ball tends to travel farther in warm air than in cooler air. Humid air, which has a lot of water vapor in it, is also less dense than dry air when they are the same temperature. This is because molecules of water vapor weigh less than molecules of oxygen and nitrogen, the two most common components of air. The more water molecules are in the air, the less dense it is, and the less friction it puts on the baseball. So if players want to hit home runs, they hope for high altitude, wind blowing out, and warm, humid air.

CHAPTER 6

Out in Left Field— The Science of Catching a Baseball

In a baseball game, the pitcher's job is to fool the batter into striking out or getting a weak hit. The batter's job is to read the pitch and swing the bat at the right time and location to get the best possible contact on the ball. When that happens, the fielders go to work. Their job is to judge the speed and location of the batted ball, get to it quickly, and get the ball back into the infield as quickly as possible to prevent the runner from getting to first base safely. Former New York Giants second baseman Bill Rigney said, "We should remember that with everything there is in the game of baseball, the thing there's the most of are outs. That makes it pretty important to catch the ball and know what to do with it after you've caught it."[18] Just as in pitching and hitting, science, especially physics, is involved with the skills of catching the ball. Well-developed skills involving the eyes, brain, and body are necessary to catch the baseball successfully.

The Science of Catching

Several factors determine where the ball will go once it is hit and how fast it will get there. The speed and location of the pitch, the swing of the bat, the spin on the ball, the temperature,

and the air resistance all affect the ball's flight path, or trajectory. Fielders must know how to make rapid judgments about how the ball comes off the bat and where the ball is going, and react quickly to those judgments.

Fielders have to know how to handle balls hit on the ground and in the air. Balls hit on the ground behave differently from balls hit in the air, and different forces act on them. A quick reaction time is needed to get in front of the ball before it gets by, to get it in the glove, transfer it to the throwing hand, and throw it quickly to the right place to get the out. Infielders ready themselves by standing with their knees slightly bent and their weight shifted forward as the pitch is made. This allows them to move quickly in any direction in response to a grounder coming their way. If there is time, the fielder will "round the ball," which means taking a few steps toward the ball and then moving slightly to the right (for a right-handed thrower) so that the ball is fielded near the left foot. With their weight already on the left foot, fielders can then take a step or a short hop toward first base on the right foot, and their momentum will carry them forward toward first base, which helps them throw smoothly and quickly.

Since baseballs have a certain amount of elasticity, they bounce when they hit the ground. It can be a challenge for

St. Louis Cardinals shortstop Julio Lugo fields a grounder during a 2009 game in Philadelphia. Infielders must ready themselves as the pitch is made so that they can move in any direction in response to the ball's movement.

Evolution of the Baseball Glove

In the early days of baseball, players wore no gloves at all. Once batters began hitting the ball harder, however, more players decided to wear protection for their hands. The first gloves looked more like today's batting gloves than fielder's gloves. The fingers were uncovered, and the palm of the glove had only a little padding. Some players made their gloves from old mittens, which is where the word "mitt" comes from. By the end of the 1870s, most players wore gloves. The first specialized mitt was a catcher's mitt created by New York Giants catcher Buck Ewing in the 1880s.

Early gloves were made of horsehide, cowhide, or buckskin. One of the most important improvements was made in 1920, when webbing was added to the space between the thumb and first finger to form a pocket for catching the ball. Since then, glove manufacturers have created different styles of webbing. Pitchers like a closed web because it helps them conceal their grip on the ball from the batter. Some infielders, such as former Cardinals shortstop Ozzie Smith, like the "sixth finger" web style, in which the webbing looks like it has a sixth finger sewn into it between the thumb and index finger.

Today, gloves are specialized for different positions. Outfielders use large gloves with long fingers for maximum reach on fly balls. Infielders use smaller gloves so they can get the ball out of the glove faster for the throw to first base. First basemen and catchers use mitts designed without individual fingers for catching those 90-mile- (144.84-km-) per-hour fastballs or for scooping bad throws out of the dirt.

Baseball gloves have evolved greatly during the many years of baseball. Today, gloves are specialized for different positions, like this catcher's mitt, which has been designed without individual fingers and is better able to catch a pitcher's fastball.

a fielder to "read" the bounce to know where the ball will be when it gets to him and where to position his glove to make a clean catch. Balls bounce differently on the dirt of the infield than they do on the grass. Dirt is harder than grass, so when the ball hits, its surface is compressed more than it is on grass. The ball's elasticity then causes it to rebound, or bounce, more than it does on the softer grass surface. Also, grass, because of its thickness and rough texture, puts more friction on a rolling ball than dirt does. The added resistance slows the ball down. Fielders know this, so they move toward the ball faster if it is rolling on grass than if it is rolling on dirt.

Catching the Ball in the Air

The ball hit in the air can come at the fielder in an almost infinite number of ways. A hard line drive will travel in a flat, straight trajectory and can get to an infielder in less than a second. A pop-up may go almost straight up off the bat. Most balls hit in the air, however, travel upward for a while before gravity pulls them back down. The fielder must judge

A fielder trying to catch a pop-up ball must judge both the speed and the trajectory of the ball in order to be at the point where the ball is within his reach to catch it before it hits the ground.

both the speed and the trajectory of the ball to be at the point where the ball is within reach in time to catch it before it hits the ground.

The trajectory of a fly ball is curved somewhat like the arc of a rainbow, but the shape of the curve is a little different. While the curve of a rainbow is a half circle, the trajectory of a fly ball follows a path called a "parabola." A parabola is a curve used in advanced mathematics, but examples of it can be seen in everyday situations. Besides a fly ball, other examples of a parabola are the path formed by the stream of water coming out of a fountain, the shape of the light cast by a flashlight, and the beautiful arc of the St. Louis Gateway Arch.

One exception to the parabolic path is the pop-up that goes vertically up behind home plate. These hits go almost straight up because of the huge amount of backspin put on them from the batter hitting the ball hard, but undercutting it. They are especially difficult to catch because, unlike other fly balls, they do not follow the typical parabolic trajectory, nor do they go straight up, then straight back down again. Because of the excessive backspin, the Magnus force on these hits create a trajectory that is, at first, curved backwards toward the backstop in a very steep path upward, until they reach the peak of their trajectory. At that point, gravity takes over, and the Magnus force reverses direction and actually causes the ball to loop back on itself and cross its own upward path on its way back down, like a stunt flier doing a loop-the-loop. Inexperienced fielders who believe they have positioned themselves properly underneath such a ball may find themselves completely fooled when the ball actually curves away from them as it approaches the ground.

Judging Trajectory

A good deal of research has been done on how a fielder learns to predict the path of a fly ball. Yale physicist Dr. Robert Adair believes that one important clue for the fielder is the sound that is produced as the bat contacts the ball. "Sometimes the difference between the sharp acoustic crack-of-the-bat [acoustics is the science of sound] and a sullen acoustic clunk-of-the-bat can be worth a run or two,"[19] he says. If the hitter connects solidly with the ball, a "crack" sound is caused by air being suddenly forced out between the ball and the bat. "If you don't hit the ball squarely you hear the bat vibrate," says Dr. Adair. "That produces a thudlike sound that gives an experienced player a clue that the ball hasn't been hit too well."[20] He says that sound reaches the fielder 1.7 seconds before visual cues indicate the flight of the ball. In that short period of time, the fielder can run about 50 feet (15.24m), an important advantage in getting to the ball on time. Baltimore Orioles outfielder Melvin Mora agrees. If he hears the crack, he runs farther out. A clunk, and he moves closer in. "As soon as I hear the sound of the bat, I know where the ball is going," he says. "It's about reaction. It's something I can't explain."[21]

The task for the outfielder is to judge two things: the steepness of the angle at which the ball is rising and the velocity of the ball. This information gives the fielder some idea of how far the ball will go. A ball that comes off the bat at a steep angle will go higher into the air than a ball that comes off the bat at a lower angle. If both hits have the same velocity and if there is little resistance from wind, the higher hit ball will not travel quite as far as the ball with lower trajectory because more of its kinetic energy is used to go up rather than out. This tells the fielder whether to move in or out. The ball with more velocity will travel farther because it has more kinetic energy overcoming gravity than the ball with less velocity. This gives fielders some indication of how much time they have to get to the ball.

It is more difficult for fielders to judge balls that are hit right toward them than balls that are hit to the right or left.

BATTER'S BOX
Sound Effects
The "crack" of the bat is the sound of about one hundred cubic centimeters (cc) of air being forced out from between the bat and the ball in about one two-thousandth of a second.

This is because there is less visual information coming to the fielders. If the ball is hit right at them, they can see it go up, but they cannot as accurately judge the steepness of the angle at which it comes off the bat. It is also harder to judge the velocity of the ball if it is coming straight toward them. They know that they do not have to move right or left to catch the ball, but it is more difficult to judge how far in or out they must move to meet the ball. If a ball is hit right or left, fielders can judge the velocity and the angle at which it is rising, and this gives them important visual information for judging where the ball will come down.

Optical Acceleration Cancellation

Even though it is more difficult, fielders still manage to catch fly balls hit directly at them more often than not. Physicist Seville Chapman, devised a theory to explain how fielders catch this kind of hit. He calls the theory "Optical Acceleration Cancellation," or OAC. He theorizes that as fielders move their position forward or backward, the rate at which the ball moves through their field of vision speeds up or slows down. If fielders move closer to the ball, it passes through their field of vision faster. If they move too far forward, they will soon realize that the ball is rising too quickly to adjust position, and the ball will sail over their heads. If they move backward, the ball travels through their field of vision more slowly, but if they move too far back, they will not be able to adjust their positions in time to keep the ball from landing on the ground in front of them.

Rather than run to where they think the ball will land and then stand there and wait for it, good fielders constantly make forward or backward adjustments to their positions so that the ball maintains a constant speed as it moves through their visual field. University of Missouri psychologist Dr. Mike Stadler, author of *The Psychology of Baseball*, explains,

> By "controlling" the way the ball moves across the image [field of vision], the player can guarantee that he will arrive at the place where the ball will land at the same time as the ball. This strategy is called an "error nulling" strategy because the player's movement is determined

"The Catch"

Throughout the history of baseball, countless memorable defensive plays have been made by outfielders, but one particular play might be the best known among baseball fans. It is simply known as "The Catch."

It was the top of the eighth inning in Game One of the 1954 World Series between the New York Giants and Cleveland Indians. With two runners on base, Cleveland's Vic Wertz came to the plate. On the fourth pitch, he connected solidly and sent the ball far into deep center field. Giants center fielder Willie Mays had been playing shallow, and when he saw how the ball was flying, he turned and ran hard straight toward the center field wall. At the warning track, and without turning around, he caught the ball over his shoulder, looking more like a football player catching a long pass. Larry Doby, the runner on second, had taken off as soon as the ball was hit, never dreaming that it would be caught. Mays spun around and fired the ball back in to second base, his momentum causing him to fall to the ground, and doubling off Doby, who had already rounded third on his way to home.

Mays himself would say later that he did not consider "The Catch" to be his best defensive play. It may be as memorable as it is because it was a World Series game or because it was one of the first

New York Giants outfielder Willie Mays is best remembered by baseball fans for one particular play simply known as "The Catch," which he made during Game One of the 1954 World Series.

games broadcast on television in the very early days of TV.

In 2006 University of Illinois at Urbana-Champaign physicist Dr. Alan Nathan reported that if the air temperature had been one degree warmer that day, "The Catch" would never have happened. Because of lower resistance of warmer air, the ball would have traveled two more inches (5.08cm)—just out of the reach of Mays' glove.

by the ball. If the ball strays from its trajectory (say, because of wind resistance), then the fielder will have to change his movement in sync with the changes in the ball's movement to keep it progressing in the same way through his field of view. So the system is assumed to employ a feedback loop: Monitor the optical acceleration. If it is increasing, slow down. If it is increasing, speed up. Repeat.[22]

Linear Optical Trajectory

If the ball is hit to the right or the left of the fielder, rather than directly at him, the player can see the actual arc of the ball's rise and see how fast it is moving. This added visual information increases the chances that the fielder will get to the ball in time to catch it. Building on the earlier work involving OAC, former NASA scientist Michael McBeath developed another theory of catching fly balls called "Linear Optical Trajectory," or LOT. LOT is similar to OAC in that the fielder still uses the path of the ball through his line of vision to make adjustments to his own path of movement, but it adds the side-to-side dimension as well as the vertical dimension

Both OAC and LOT describe what information the eyes perceive and send to the brain for processing. How that information is processed in the brain and how it leads to a physical response is not known for sure, but two theories are debated among scientists—Information Processing (IP) and Ecological Psychology (EP).

Information Processing Theory

The IP theory of human perception and processing compares the human brain to a computer. The senses send input from all life experiences to the brain, where information is stored in a memory system. The brain also has a "main processor" that takes new input and combines it with data already in memory to solve new problems as they arise. This is how people know, for example, that if their senses tell the brain that they are cold, they have several alternatives to solve the problem, from putting on a coat to turning up the heat or having a warm drink.

Applied to catching a fly ball, IP theory suggests that the fielder's sense of sight sends information about the flight of the ball to the brain, where the information is combined with previously stored data about all the fly balls caught in the past, to enable the fielder to decide how to move to catch this particular ball.

Ecological Psychology

The other theory about human perception is Ecological Psychology, or EP. EP theory eliminates the need to call information up from memory. When applied to baseball, EP proponents argue that the fielder does not need to rely on stored memory but can make decisions based on information from OAC or LOT alone.

There is still a lot of discussion about which theory, if either, is more accurate for explaining how fielders judge fly balls. "This is still up for debate," notes Bleacher Report writer Dan Peterson, "as the IPers would argue 'learned facts' like what pitch was thrown, how a certain batter hits those pitches, how the prevailing wind will affect the ball, etc. And, with EP, how can the skill differences between a young ballplayer and an experienced major leaguer be accounted for? What is the point of practice, if the trials and errors are not stored/accessed in memory?"[23]

Regardless of which theory explains it best, there is no doubt that fielding the ball well requires a great deal of practice. With proper training, coaching, experience, perseverance, and an understanding of the science behind it, fielding is a skill that all ball players can master at one level or another.

CHAPTER 7

"Ninety Percent of This Game Is Half Mental"— The Psychology of Baseball

Physical strength and skill are essential for succeeding at baseball, but they are not enough. Success in baseball also requires focus, confidence, and mental toughness—"inner" skills that cannot be coached. Psychologist Dr. Mike Stadler says, "Baseball is impossible without psychology: impossible to play, and impossible to appreciate fully as a fan."[24] Hall of Fame pitcher Tom Seaver agrees. "The difference between the physical abilities of the players in the major leagues is not that great," he says, "and the difference between the teams is not that great. So what it comes down to is that the dividing factor between the team that wins and the one that loses is the mental attitude, the effort they give, the mental alertness that keeps them from making mental mistakes. The concentration and the dedication are the deciding factors."[25]

Psychology in baseball is so important that it can cause a superstar athlete to experience a meltdown so sudden and so profound that it can delay, alter, or even end a career. The pressure to succeed, and to keep on succeeding, can put so much stress on an eighteen-year-old star pitcher drafted right out of high school that the young player may suddenly be unable to find the strike zone, or it may cause a veteran slugger to suddenly go hitless for weeks at a time. Stresses off the field also can interfere with players' ability to focus to the point that their physical skills seem to abandon them.

Psychology not only affects the players. Fans in the bleachers behave according to their own set of expectations and beliefs. The most involved fans invest so much emotional energy in their team that a loss in an important game can cause an emotional funk that can last for days. Their behavior in the stands, whether cheers or boos, can, in turn, have a psychological impact on the performance and behavior of the players.

The Baseball Personality

What makes two players of comparable ability come to the major leagues and have very different experiences in terms of success? Dr. Stadler describes what he calls "the baseball personality." In 1980 the New York Mets drafted two players whose athletic abilities were similar—Daryl Strawberry and Billy Beane. When Strawberry began playing for the major league team in May 1983, he struggled to say the least. By July his batting average had dropped to below .200. Then one day he came up to the plate in the eighth inning of a tie game. Despite his poor performance so far in the season and the high-pressure situation he found himself in, he did not doubt his ability. "I thought about hitting one out of the park and winning the game," he told reporters. And so he did. "I've always got the confidence," he told them. "I know I'm going to hit plenty more in situations like that."[26] He went on to hit twenty-six home runs that year and was named Rookie of the Year.

Beane, however, had a very different experience. Once in the major leagues, the pressure seemed to be too much for him, and his talent disappeared. In his book *Moneyball*, author Michael Lewis wrote, "Inside a batter's box he

Although he struggled during the first half of his rookie year, New York Mets player Daryl Strawberry had the confidence to eventually succeed as a professional baseball player.

experienced a kind of claustrophobia. The batter's box was a cage designed to crush his spirit."[27] Beane's playing career lasted only six years and ended with a .219 batting average and only three home runs.

The Athletic Motivation Inventory

Confidence like Daryl Strawberry's is a personality trait that is important for the future success of a baseball player. In 1973 psychologist William Winslow began using a psychological

The Sports Psychologist

Psychologists are health professionals who specialize in the diagnosis and treatment of various kinds of mental and emotional disorders, such as anxiety and stress. They may work in schools, hospitals, clinics, or for large companies. Although they are not medical doctors, they are highly trained in their field. In some states a Master's Degree is required to become a psychologist, and in others, a doctoral degree is required. Psychologists must be licensed in the state in which they practice.

Sports psychologists specialize in working with athletes, especially those at the college, professional, and Olympic levels. They may work with a team organization or with an individual athlete. They may also be involved in research or teaching. Sports psychologists focus on helping the athlete achieve his or her maximum potential by building confidence, dealing with outside stresses, and coping with sudden success or failure. Research shows that sports psychologists can help injured athletes heal faster using techniques such as guided imagery (using the imagination to mentally "visualize" a desired outcome) and self-hypnosis.

Currently few formal education programs exist specifically for sports psychology, although some psychology programs offer classes in the field. A psychologist interested in sports psychology can gain experience by working in the specialty and can become certified by professional organizations such the Association for the Advancement of Applied Sports Psychology (AAASP).

test specifically designed to measure personality traits such as confidence in prospective professional baseball players. He called it the Athletic Motivation Inventory (AMI). Professional scouts and team managers use the test to help them recruit players. Prospects who scored high on the test were considered to possess a range of traits that indicated a high probability of success.

The eleven traits on the AMI fall into two broad categories—attitudinal and emotional. Attitudinal traits are those that may change over time. An example of an attitudinal trait is drive or ambition (how badly athletes want to succeed and how hard they will work to succeed). Other examples are coachability (how much the athlete respects and listens to coaches or other leadership), how much the athlete wants to set an example for teammates, whether the athlete wants to take part in decision making, and how much the athlete trusts other teammates. Emotional traits are a more fundamental part of the athlete's personality and are not likely to change over time. These include such things as aggression, confidence, mental toughness, emotional control in difficult situations, and taking responsibility for one's own behavior.

Team Chemistry

One question that has been asked by sports psychologists such as Dr. Stadler is how these personality traits translate into success for a team. "Do teams that succeed have a mix of leaders and followers?" he asks. "Are successful teams made up of largely conscientious and responsible players? We need a study that asks 'All other things being equal, do teams with certain mixes of personality traits fare better than others?'"[28]

The way in which team members relate to each other and treat each other has been referred to as team chemistry, or team cohesion. Good team chemistry means that the team

The New York Yankees celebrate after winning the 2009 World Series. Although the Yankees have won more World Series than any other team, the club is not a particularly cohesive one with high-profile conflicts between team members dating back several years.

members work together to achieve a common goal, respect each other, and support each other even during times of failure or other stress. Research has suggested that team cohesion is related to a team's success on the field, and this would seem to make sense. If a group of people get along together, it follows that they would succeed more often.

In baseball, however, that is not necessarily true. The New York Yankees have seen an enormous amount of success over their lifetime, having won more World Series than any other team, despite being known as not particularly cohesive. High-profile conflicts between team members date back to the 1920s and include intense feuds between Babe Ruth and Lou Gehrig. Talented, but difficult, stars such as Leo Durocher, Billy Martin, and Reggie Jackson have created some bad publicity. "So much of psychology and sociology emphasizes the importance of communicating and creating strong bonds to improve group performance, but in a lot of situations that is just not how it works,"[29] says Dr. Calvin Morrill, professor of sociology at the University of California, Irvine.

The true importance of team chemistry becomes clearer if the two different kinds of cohesion are studied. Success is related to which type of cohesion exists on the team. First is task cohesion. This means that the team can function effectively as a group on the field to achieve a goal—winning games. They cooperate with each other to reach the goal, regardless of how well they get along with each other. When a catcher trots out to the mound to collaborate with the pitcher on how to deal with a particular batter or when a shortstop, second baseman, and first baseman know each other's skills well enough to turn a clean double play, they are showing good task cohesion.

The other type of team cohesion is social cohesion. This means that the players are friends outside of the ballpark and enjoy spending time together as well as playing baseball together. As the experience of the Yankees demonstrates, good social cohesion has less

BATTER'S BOX
18 Years Old

The age of baseball legend Joe DiMaggio in 1933 when he had a sixty-one-game hitting streak for the minor league San Francisco Seals.

to do with the team's success than does task cohesion. In fact, it can even cause problems if a conflict arises that drives a wedge between teammates that affects their task cohesion.

Streaks and Slumps

From May 16 until July 17, 1941, New York Yankee Joe DiMaggio got at least one base hit in fifty-six consecutive games, the longest hitting streak in major league history. There have been fifty-three times when a player has had a hitting streak that lasted at least thirty games. Conversely, although not officially recorded, most players have experienced slumps, times when they may go several games and not get on base at all. Streaks and slumps are a natural part of the game of baseball, but are they real, or nothing more than just good or bad luck?

Fans and the media tend to get caught up in the excitement of a player who is in the middle of a hitting streak, but fans do not necessarily take into account many variables that affect whether or not the hitter gets a base hit. Confidence, concentration, and skill certainly play a part in hitting success, but it is more complicated than that. Dr. Mike Stadler explains, "One potential problem...is that simply looking at whether or not an at bat resulted in a hit is to look past how well the ball was hit. A lazy infield pop-up and a line drive that knocks down the third baseman and breaks three bones in his glove hand both go into the scorebook as outs. A sizzling line drive up the middle and a bloop over the second baseman's head both [score] as hits. So...the result depends to some extent on the quality of the contact...and to some extent on luck."[30] Other factors—the defensive skill of the other team, the skill of the pitcher, the time of day or night, home game or away game—all factor into the player's chances during any particular at bat.

Hitting slumps, though, may have more to do with psychological forces. Sometimes a player is not hitting well because of a mechanical problem with his swing or his stance. Other times, however, the player may be having trouble concentrating or remaining focused on the task at hand, especially if things going on in his life distract him from the game.

Good players who are slumping may lose confidence in their abilities, and failure becomes even more likely as they start to believe that they have lost their skills. This depends a lot, though, on the players' attitudes—how much of the trouble they attribute to loss of skill and how much they decide is just bad luck. In 1983 a reporter for *The New York Times* asked Joe Morgan about his 0-for-35 hitting slump. "But I'm not in a slump," Morgan replied. "I'm just not getting base hits. There's a difference. A slump is when you're not hitting the ball and striking out. I've been hitting the ball; they're just making great catches."[31] Morgan understood that a real slump has more to do with how well and how often the ball is hit than how often the batter is reaching first base.

Getting out of a slump can be difficult for a ballplayer. One high school player offers this advice: "The most important thing I tell myself is to hit like I know I can and to have fun at the plate. Baseball is a game of the little things and confidence is huge. Even the best players in the world struggle sometimes, but what makes them the best is how they come back from a slump or bad game and focus on the current at bat. This idea is key and if one can manage all this, they will play the best of their ability."[32]

Clutch and Choke—Coping With Pressure

Certain situations in a game are more important than others. The ninth inning of the last game of the World Series with the score tied, bases loaded, and two outs might be one of the most pressure-filled situations a pitcher or hitter can face. Millions of people are watching, and the outcome of the entire World Series depends on what the player does right here and right now. Whether the player succeeds or "chokes" in this "clutch" situation hinges mostly on how that player handles pressure.

> ## BATTER'S BOX
> ### Bad Behavior!
> In June 2009 fans at a high school baseball game in Iowa became so unruly that the umpire ejected the entire crowd.

Pressure is put on baseball players in many different ways. They always face pressure to live up to the expectations of coaches, teammates, and fans, not to mention themselves, especially for highly touted rookies who feel the need to prove themselves. If the game is an important one, pressure to perform is greater for all the players, but especially for the stars. For the pros, negotiating a new contract or the fear of being traded may affect performance. For younger players, parents can put a great deal of pressure on them to get that hit or make that catch and get that college scholarship.

All players, at one time or another, get the opportunity to perform in a "clutch" situation. Some players seem to thrive on pressure like this. For them, the pressure actually makes them play better. They are able to remain calm, focused, and intent on the task at hand as if this at bat were like any other. These players get a reputation for being clutch players. For others, the same pressure can cause them to choke.

Choking under pressure seems to be a more common occurrence than performing in the clutch. High-pressure situations may cause players who doubt their own abilities to overthink the mechanics of their swing or pitch and become overly aware of the details of those mechanics. This kind of self-focus, commonly called "trying too hard," means paying too much attention to skills that normally come naturally to the player. It may cause a change in mechanics and adversely affect performance. The younger player who is struggling with this may be tempted to spend more time at practice, but this can sometimes contribute to the overthinking that caused the trouble in the first place. Arizona State coach Rob Gray says, "If we force you to go back and think about each stage of what you're doing, you actually start interfering with this procedural knowledge, this motor memory, and you start messing it up. It's like tinkering with a machine that's running really efficiently. You start trying to control everything

Young pitchers who are faced with high-pressure situations during games may choke under pressure. As a result they may change the mechanics of their pitching and adversely affect their performance.

yourself and it messes it up and it hurts your performance."[33] Another way that ballplayers might deal with pressure to perform is by having and sticking to superstitions.

Superstitions and Jinxes

Baseball players are known to be among the most superstitious of all athletes, and have been since the earliest days of the game. Third baseman Wade Boggs ate only fried chicken before a game. Houston Astros second baseman Craig Biggio never washed his batting helmet the entire season. Pitcher Turk Wendell brushed his teeth and then chewed licorice between every inning. Some players refuse to step on the foul line as they take the field; others make a point of stepping on it. Many players feel an almost obsessive need to keep the same jersey numbers they have had since Little League.

Many superstitions begin when a player has a particularly good day on the field and then goes over everything that happened that day to establish a cause-and-effect relationship between the behavior and the success. If the player did anything different, ate something new, or listened to a particular song, it can become an instant superstition.

Athletes who have these superstitions believe strongly that sticking to them will influence their performance for the better. Sports psychology tends to bear that out. Anything that gives a player a little boost in confidence and that supports a belief in success can contribute to realizing that success.

A jinx is the superstitious belief that something someone says or does can cause a player to fail. For example, no one in the dugout will speak to a pitcher who is working on a no-hitter, or even talk about it, for fear of "jinxing" the pitcher. This extends to fans, sportscasters, and even people watching on TV. Sports announcers may think that they might jinx a batter if they mention the hitting streak the batter is in at the moment, or they might jinx a pitcher by mentioning that the pitcher has not given up a home run in the last ten starts.

Curse of the Billy Goat

Superstitions abound in baseball, but they are taken to their extreme in the form of "curses." The "Curse of the Bambino" was said to be the Boston Red Sox's punishment for selling Babe Ruth to the New York Yankees after the 1919 season and the reason the Boston Red Sox had not won a World Series since 1918. (The "curse" was broken when they won the series in 2004.)

The Chicago Cubs have not won a World Series since 1908, a longer dry spell than any other major league team. According to baseball lore, this is because of the "Curse of the Billy Goat." In 1945 the Cubs played the Detroit Tigers in the World Series. After the first three games, the Cubs led two games to one. At game four, tavern owner and Cubs fan William Sianis showed up at the game with his pet goat Murphy. During the game, it rained briefly, and, when the sun came out again, the warmth sent the odor of wet goat throughout the stands. After fans complained, Wrigley Field security guards kicked out Sianis and Murphy. Furious, Sianis stood outside the park and shouted that never again would another World Series game be played there. The Cubs went on to lose that game and the series. Although they have come close on several occasions, they have not made it back to the World Series since that day.

Psychology in the Stands

Psychology in baseball is not limited to the athletes on the playing field. Almost as long as there has been baseball, baseball fans in the stands have been rooting for "their" team. Today, almost 70 million fans attend baseball games each year. Baseball fans have their own set of psychological factors that influence their behavior.

According to Dr. Mike Stadler, author of *The Psychology of Baseball*, people become fans by a process called "socialization," in which a person adopts a set of beliefs and customs held by a particular group. Baseball fans become socialized into the baseball "culture" by identifying with a particular team, wearing the team's colors, knowing statistics about the players and the team, and participating in baseball rituals like singing "Take Me Out to the Ball Game" in the seventh inning. Identifying with a team provides a sense of belonging and acceptance in a group. Even perfect strangers might become fast friends by the end of a game simply by sharing their enthusiasm for their team and experiencing an emotionally charged event together.

Sports psychologists study fan psychology because it can explain certain fan behaviors. After a loss, for example, the casual fan might feel disappointed for awhile, but the die-hard fanatic may feel depressed or angry for days, especially if the game was particularly important or if the loss was to a strong rival team. This fan may even behave in a hostile or aggressive way toward the other team's fans or players during the game. Former Cardinal outfielder J.D. Drew was pelted with batteries by Philadelphia Phillies fans after he left their team to sign with St. Louis. At other times fan behavior can provoke a hostile response from an athlete. In 2004 Texas Rangers pitcher Frank Francisco was arrested after he responded to fan's taunting by throwing a bullpen chair into the stands, breaking a woman's nose.

Most baseball fans, however, are not naturally violent people. They go to games and root for their team mainly to be entertained. For most fans, strong team identification might make the game more entertaining and exciting, but even if their team is on the losing side of a bad season, they go for other reasons—because they love the game itself, because it takes them back to their own childhood for a few hours, or because they want to pass that love to their own children. Even someone who does not identify with a team and knows little to nothing about baseball may find that it is fun to go to the ballpark on a warm summer evening and watch a game of baseball—America's national pastime.

NOTES

Chapter 1: America's Pastime—The Story of Baseball

1. Quoted in Mark Newman, "Why We Love Baseball," *MLB.com*, February 14, 2007. Available online at http://mlb.mlb.com/news/article.jsp?ymd=20070213&content_id=1800838&vkey=news_mlb&fext=.jsp&c_id=mlb.
2. Newman, "Why We Love Baseball."
3. Quoted in "10K Truth Baseball Quotes." Available online at http://www.10ktruth.com/the_quotes/baseball.htm.
4. Quoted in Richard Nordquist, "The Language of Baseball," *About.com*, 2009. Available online at http://grammar.about.com/od/words/a/baseballjargon.htm.
5. Newman, "Why We Love Baseball."

Chapter 2: Power Hitters and Cannon Arms—Training and Conditioning

6. Tony Burtt, "Baseball Strength Training," *Be a Better Hitter.com*. Available online at http://www.bea-betterhitter.com/text/conditioning/strengthtraining/baseballstregthtraining.htm.
7. Jason R. Karp, "Muscle Fiber Types and Training," *Coachr.org*. Available online at http://www.coachr.org/fiber.htm.
8. Donald A. Chu, *Jumping Into Plyometrics*. Champaign, IL: Human Kinetics Publishers, Inc., 1998, pg. 1.
9. Charles Slavik, "Training Differences of Baseball Players vs. Other Athletes," *Coach John Peters' Baseball Tips*. Available online at http://baseballtips.com/playertraining.html.

Chapter 3: Tommy John Elbow—Baseball Injuries

10. Quoted in "Orthopedic Experts Examine Baseball Throwing Injuries," *Medical News Today*, April 9, 2009. Available online at http://www.medicalnewstoday.com/articles/145703.php.
11. Quoted in "Smith Breaks Leg Sliding to a Base," *The New York Times*, October 7, 1914. Available online at http://query.nytimes.com/gst/abstract.html?res=9A0CE5D71638E633A25754C0A9669D946596D

6CF&scp=145&sq=October+7%2C+1914&st=p.

12. Quoted in "Orthopedic Experts Examine Baseball Throwing Injuries."

Chapter 4: Curves, Sliders, and Knuckleballs— The Science of Pitching

13. Quoted in Porter Johnson, "The Physics of Baseball," *Illinois Institute of Technology*. Available online at http://www.iit.edu/~johnsonp/smart00/lesson3.htm.

14. Quoted in Carl T. Hall, "A Neophyte Takes on the Science of Pitching," *San Francisco Chronicle*, July 9, 2007. Available online at http://articles.sfgate.com/2007-07-09/news/17253497_1_hitting-san-francisco-s-exploratorium-baseball-expert.

Chapter 5: "Swing and a Long One!"—When the Bat Meets the Ball

15. "Yogi Berra Quotes," *Baseball Almanac*. Available online at http://www.baseball-almanac.com/quotes/quoberra.shtml.

16. Quoted in "There's More Than Meets the Eye to Catching a Fly Ball in the Outfield," *University of New Hampshire*, April 10, 2006. Available online at http://www.unh.edu/news/news_releases/2006/april/lw_060410ball.html.

17. Quoted in Noel Wanner, "How Far Can You Hit One?: The Science of Baseball," *Exploratorium*. Available online at http://www.exploratorium.edu/baseball/howfar.html.

Chapter 6: Out in Left Field—The Science of Catching a Baseball

18. Quoted in H. A. Dorfman and Karl Kuehl, *The Mental Game of Baseball*. Lanham, MD: Diamond Communications, 1995, pg. 312.

19. Quoted in Harald Franzen, "Baseball Bat Cracks and Clunks Tell Outfielder Where to Go," *Scientific American*, June 11, 2001. Available online at http://www.scientificamerican.com/article.cfm?id=baseball-bat-cracks-and-c.

20. Quoted in "Crack! Clunk! Physicists—and Players—Tune in to the Sound of Baseball," *The Free Library*, May 6, 2002. Available online at http://www.thefreelibrary.com/Crack!+Clunk!+Physicists--and+players--tune+in+to+the+sounds+of...-a086170479.

21. Quoted in James Glanz, "The Crack of the Bat: Acoustics Takes on the Sounds of Baseball," *The New York Times*, June 26, 2001. Available online at http://www.nytimes.com/2001/06/26/science/the-crack-of-the-bat-acoustics-takes-on-the-sound-of-baseball.html.

22. Mike Stadler, *The Psychology of Baseball: Inside the Mental Game of Major League Players*. New York: Gotham, 2008, pg. 54.

23. Dan Peterson, "Baseball Brains—Fielding into the World Series," *Sports Are 80 Percent Mental*, October 19, 2008. Available online at http://blog.80percentmental.com/2008/10/baseball-brains-fielding-into-world.html.

Chapter 7: "Ninety Percent of This Game Is Half Mental"—The Psychology of Baseball

24. Stadler, pg. x.
25. Dorfman and Kuehl, pg. 1.
26. Stadler, pg. 120.
27. Stadler, pg. 120.
28. Stadler, pg. 134.
29. Quoted in Benedict Carey, "Close Doesn't Always Count in Winning Games," *The New York Times*, March 7, 2005. Available online at http://www.nytimes.com/2005/03/07/sports/baseball/07psych.html.
30. Stadler, pg. 148.
31. Quoted in Dorfman and Kuehl, pg. 217.
32. Quoted in Bill Mooney, "What to Do while Getting Out of a Slump." Available online at http://www.bioforcebaseball.com/tips_and_articles/tag/hitting-slump.
33. Quoted in "The Psychology of Baseball," *Physorg*, March 31, 2007. Available online at http://www.physorg.com/news94554127.html.

athletic motivation inventory (AMI): A psychological test used to measure personality traits that can predict success in baseball.

ballistic stretching: A method of stretching muscles that adds a series of small bounces to the stretch.

ballistics: A method of training that maximizes power by applying a high amount of force to a low amount of weight and eliminates the need to expend energy by slowing and stopping the movement.

Bernoulli's principle: Principle of aerodynamics that states that the faster air moves over the surface of an object, the less pressure it places on the object.

concentric action: The phase of plyometric exercise during which the muscle contracts and applies its force.

conservation of momentum: A physical principle that states that momentum created in a moving object remains the same even when that momentum is transferred to another object.

dynamic stretching: A method of stretching muscles that includes moving them through the joint's range of motion.

eccentric action: The pre-stretch phase of plyometric exercise during which the muscle builds and stores energy in preparation for contraction.

ecological psychology: A theory about human perception that states that human beings can make decisions based on information at hand without the need to call it up from memory.

elasticity: A physical property that describes how quickly the surface of an object returns to its original shape after being compressed.

electrolytes: Essential chemicals in the body that are necessary for the proper functioning of all the body's cells and systems.

fast-twitch fibers: Muscle fibers that contract more quickly and grow larger than slow-twitch fibers, but have less endurance.

force: Any outside stress that causes an object to move or change its shape.

force-velocity relationship: An equation used to measure power. Power equals force times distance, divided by time.

friction: The resistance put on a moving object by another surface that causes it to slow down.

impingement: Overuse injury characterized by pressure placed on a nerve or blood vessel.

information processing theory: A theory of human perception that likens the brain to a computer that stores sensory input in memory for future use.

kinetic energy: The form of energy involved in movement.

linear optical trajectory: A theory of how a fielder judges the trajectory of a fly ball that is hit to one side rather than straight on.

Magnus force: The force on a spinning object that causes it to change its path in flight.

mass: The amount of matter contained in an object.

momentum: A measure of how an object moves, depending on its mass and velocity, expressed in the equation momentum (p) = mass (m) $\times$ velocity (v).

motor unit: The combination of a group of muscle fibers with the nerve that makes the muscle contract.

1RM: The maximum amount of weight that a person can move one time with a particular muscle.

optical acceleration cancellation: A theory of how fielders judge the trajectory of a fly ball that is hit directly toward them.

parabola: A mathematical curve that describes the shape of the trajectory of a fly ball. A parabolic curve is wider at its base than at its top, like the arc of water coming out of a drinking fountain.

plyometrics: A method of power training that puts the muscles in a pre-stretch before executing a powerful contraction.

sequential summation of movement: A physics principle that states that conserved momentum transferred from a larger object to a smaller one will cause the smaller object to move faster than the larger object that provided the momentum.

slow-twitch fibers: Muscle fibers that contract more slowly and do not grow as large as fast-twitch fibers, but have more endurance.

social cohesion: A form of team chemistry in which players get along as friends and may socialize with each other outside the ballpark.

static stretching: Stretching a muscle with a slow movement that is held in place for twenty to thirty seconds.

strength-shortening cycle: The cycle of a plyometric exercise that includes the eccentric action (pre-stretch), a very brief pause, and a concentric action (muscle contraction).

task cohesion: A form of team chemistry in which team members work together to achieve a common goal, regardless of their personal relationship.

trajectory: The path followed by an object in flight.

trampoline effect: An action in which an object that is hit by another object becomes compressed, then springs back to its original form with minimal loss of energy.

velocity: A measure of the rate of change in position over a period of time in a particular direction.

FOR MORE INFORMATION

Books

James Bow, *Baseball Science (Sports Science)*. New York: Crabtree Publishing Company, 2009. Good overview of science related to baseball.

Dan Gutman, *The Way Baseball Works*. New York: Simon and Schuster, 1996. A heavily illustrated and comprehensive look at many aspects of the game. Good for older readers.

Keltie Thomas, *How Baseball Works*. Toronto, Canada: Maple Tree Press, 2008. A comprehensive look at many facets of baseball, including history, science, equipment, training, pitching, hitting, stories about players, and more.

Salvatore Tocci, *Experiments With Sports*. New York: Children's Press, 2003. Explores the science of sports with simple experiments using common objects.

Internet Sources

The Exploratorium, "The Science of Baseball." http://www.exploratorium.edu/baseball/ Brightly illustrated comic book-style site with information about many aspects of baseball science.

Jonathan R. Drobnis, "The Physics Behind Baseball." http://ffden-2.phys.uaf.edu/211_fall2002.web.dir/Jon_Drobnis/index.html Illustrated with photos and diagrams, this site offers easy-to-read information on the history and science of baseball.

Kevin Bonsor and Joe Martin, "How Baseball Works," *How Stuff Works*. http://entertainment.howstuffworks.com/baseball.htm From the "How Stuff Works" series, this site includes videos and links to information about the game, the equipment, rules, strategies for playing, and more.

Thinkquest.org. "Baseball: The Game and Beyond" *Oracle Education Foundation*. http://library.thinkquest.org/11902/ From Thinkquest, this site offers information about baseball and its science at a variety of levels, depending on the reader's preference. A "Trivia Ticker" offers a new fun fact every thirty seconds.

INDEX

PICTURE CREDITS

ABOUT THE AUTHOR

Lizabeth Hardman received her Bachelor of Science in Nursing from the University of Florida in 1978 and her Bachelor of Secondary Education from Southwest Missouri State University in 1991. She currently lives in Springfield, Missouri, where she works full time as a registered nurse. When not working or writing, she enjoys reading, hiking, St. Louis Cardinals baseball, and Florida Gators football. This is her sixth book for Lucent Books.